52517

HX
653
.C63

Cohen, Daniel.

Not of the world

| DATE | | | |
|---|---|---|---|
| | | | |
| | | | |
| | | | |
| | | | |
| | | | |
| | | | |
| | | | |
| | | | |
| | | | |
| | | | |
| | | | |
| | | | |

# Not of the World

# Not of the World

## A History of
## The Commune in America

DANIEL COHEN

Illustrated with engravings and photographs

 Follett Publishing Company / Chicago

## Photo Credits

John Olson, *Life Magazine* © 1969 Time Inc.: *Cover.*

James L. Ballard, from the Collection of Susan Jackson Keig: *pages 46, 74, 76. The Billings Gazette: pages 104, 105 left & right.* The Boston Society Old State House: *page 118.* The British Museum: *page 25.* Daniel Cohen: *pages 177, 180, 194.* Culver Pictures: *page 125.* Dover Publications, New York: *pages 43, 48, 49, 52, 58, 59, 96, 101, 113, 128, 134.* David Gahr: *page 170.* From the Collection of Susan Jackson Keig: *pages 51, 54–55, 60, 63, 66, 71.* Magnum Photos/Eve Arnold: *pages 164, 165.* Magnum Photos/Burk Uzzle: *page 160. The New York Times: pages 79, 169, 184–85.* Old Economy Village: *pages 85, 88.* Oneida, Ltd.: *pages 143, 153.* Pennsylvania Historical and Museum Commission, Harrisburg, Pennsylvania: *pages 30, 33, 36–37.* Linda Plett: *page 99. The Times-Herald Record: page 190.*

ISBN 0–695–40405–9 Titan binding
ISBN 0–695–80405–7 Trade binding

Library of Congress Catalog Card Number: 73–81995

*Second Printing*

To Jeannie

# Contents

# List of Illustrations

*If ye were of the world, the world would love his own: but because ye are not of the world, but I have chosen you out of the world, therefore the world hateth you. John 15:19*

# 1 ✿ The Golden Age and the Millennium

One of history's most persistent ideas—or myths—is that mankind once lived in a state of perfect and happy equality. In this state all shared without rancor or jealousy the abundant fruits of the earth. This idyllic existence, say the legends, was lost with the introduction of private property, the concept of "Mine and Thine."

The ancient Greeks called this lost Golden Age the Age of Saturn. ". . . men used to cultivate good faith and virtue spontaneously, without laws. Punishment and fear did not exist, nor were threatening phrases to be read from fixed bronze tablets," said the poet Ovid.

Whether people ever did, or could, exist in a perfectly equalitarian and communal state is unknown. Some have claimed to see communal equalitarianism in the lives of certain primitive tribes. Others say that communal living was one of the stages of mankind's social development, and that the Golden Age myths refer to a life-style from prehistoric days. Both points are arguable.

When the ancient Greeks and Romans began theorizing about a new Golden Age, it was one severely ruled by laws and by threatening phrases read from fixed bronze tablets. As far as the Greeks and Romans were concerned, the old equalitarian Age of Saturn, if it had ever existed, was gone forever.

Nearly twenty-five hundred years ago, Plato, the most influential of all the Greek philosophers, outlined his idea of a perfect state in a work called *The Republic.* Plato's perfect state is a society based upon the most nonequalitarian of all human institutions, slavery. A sort of regimented equality was supposed to exist among the rulers, but it is hardly the perfect, happy equality of the Age of Saturn. In fact, Plato based his idea of a republic largely on the grim military state of Sparta. Fifteen centuries later, the English philosopher and statesman, Sir Thomas More, recast the ideas of Plato's republic in terms of his own time and called his perfect state Utopia.

Neither Plato nor More nor most of the other theorists who envisioned ideal societies ever attempted to put their theories to the practical test. Indeed, such theories were not usually meant as practical blueprints for a future state at all. They were simply rhetorical devices with which the writer could criticize, by contrast, the defects he saw in his own society. The very name More chose for his society indicates this; "Utopia" is based on Greek words meaning "not a place" or "nowhere."

But some people did, and still do, attempt to establish equalitarian utopias on this earth. They rarely rely on the elaborate formulations of a Plato or a More. In practice, the more detailed the theory, the more disastrous the communal experiment has usually turned out to be. Most of the attempts to make a utopian society have been made by men and women of humble origins, unscholarly and even illiterate folk, whose primary desire was to return to the equalitarian simplicity that they believed existed in the lost Golden Age.

The first communal sect for which we have extensive information is the Essenes. Members of this once obscure Hebrew group lived in Palestine before the birth of Christ and have become famous in modern times as the authors of the Dead Sea Scrolls. From the Scrolls and other sources we get a picture of the Essenes, and it is not a particularly attractive one. At its height the sect had about four thousand members, all celibate males. They wore white robes and were rigid ascetics, who observed the Sabbath so obsessively that they refused even to relieve themselves on that day. They relied heavily on individual prophetic inspiration rather than a regular priesthood. Though their members were scattered throughout ancient Palestine, they somehow shared all their property, which didn't amount to very much. The Essenes generally stood apart from the mainstream of Hebrew life and belief, and they may well have had connections with some of the ascetic mystery religions and cults of Rome and Greece. The mystery sects, too, may have had communal elements, but we know little of them. The Essenes flourished briefly and then died out. Many of their beliefs were diffused through later Jewish and Christian thought, however.

Many people believe that the early Christians lived in a state of primitive communism, sharing all of their goods equally. Since this was thought to be the life of Christians at the time of the Twelve Apostles, it is often called apostolic Christianity. Certainly some of the phrases in the New Testament seem to indicate that a communitarian way of life was lived by the early followers of Jesus. Particularly influential has been this description of the early Christian community found in the Book of Acts, chapter 4, verses 32 to 35:

"And the multitude of them that believed were of one heart and of one soul: neither said any of them that ought of the things which he possessed was his own; but they had all things in common. . . . Neither was there any among them that lacked: for as many as were possessors of lands or houses sold them, and brought the prices of the things that

*Woodcut showing the imaginary island of Utopia, from an edition of Thomas More's* UTOPIA *published in 1518.*

were sold, and laid them down at the apostles' feet: and distribution was made unto every man according as he had need."

The description in Acts is quite clear, but it is probably more of a restatement of the old Golden Age myth than an accurate description of any real early Christian community. As an unpopular and often persecuted minority, Christians doubtless banded together to help one another. But no evidence exists to support the belief that there was a consistent attempt to establish a community of goods among the early Christians. The extent to which a communal society is supported by the teachings of Jesus is debatable, and certainly the early church fathers, particularly the Apostle Paul, had a conservative social outlook.

In writing to the Corinthians, Paul insisted that Christians should remain in the social situation in which God had placed them. Slaves should not be disturbed by their earthly condition or try to better it: "For he that is called in the Lord, being a servant, is the Lord's freeman: likewise also he that is called, being free, is Christ's servant." Equality, yes, but only in the eyes of the Lord. In the material world all the old economic and social inequalities were to remain unchallenged. When the Church triumphed in the Roman world, it became even more aggressively conservative in its social views. As one of the largest landowners and most powerful lords in the Western world, the Roman Church set itself firmly against revolutionary doctrines like the sharing of property.

Besides, in the view of the church fathers, any Golden Age of equality and sharing had been irrevocably lost in the Fall of Adam. Because of man's basically sinful nature, the Church held that such institutions as private property, coercive government, and even slavery were not only inevitable but necessary. Sinful man needed restraints, and without direct divine intervention the Golden Age of equality was beyond reach. Yet the dream seemed such a wonderful one that it persisted and served as a model for Christians in later ages who tried to reestablish a Golden Age on earth. Some felt that communal living was a necessity for Christians, just as it had been in the days of the Apostles.

It was not to the past alone that many Christians looked for an equalitarian Golden Age; they believed that another Golden Age was about to dawn at any moment. The very early Christians deeply and truly felt that the world was in its Last Days. The New Testament bristles with phrases indicating how sure Christians were that Christ would return, and the world as they knew it would come to an end within their own lifetime. Revelations concerning the return of Christ and the final judgement of mankind are called apocalyptic. Apocalyptic feelings were so strong among early Christians that they displayed a notable lack of interest in social matters. What difference did it make if a man were free or a slave, since the world as they knew it was going to end any day—indeed, at any hour.

Just exactly what was going to happen when Christ returned was never entirely clear. It was popularly held that the return of Christ would mark the dawning of the millennium, a thousand-year period in which Christ and his saints would reign over the earth. During the millennium men would again return to that state of perfect peace and equality that they had lost after the Fall.

Apocalyptic movements and writings proliferated among Christians for the first century after Jesus. But gradually the belief grew that the millennium was going to be delayed, that it was a remote rather than an imminent event. Yet few doubted that in time it would arrive. And many Christians believed, and still believe, that the millennium will come within their own lifetime.

It might seem paradoxical that a belief that the world as we know it is about to end would inspire people to establish a new social order in that world. Yet historically most communal sects have held profoundly apocalyptic or millennial, beliefs.

There are two reasons behind the apparent paradox. First, since the millennium was generally expected to be an era of equality and sharing, the communitarians felt that they would be getting a jump on the rest of mankind, and that their actions would be most pleasing to God. Many even believed that the establishment of their particular society would be the signal that would usher in the millennium. Their movement, they thought, would sweep the world, banishing selfishness and hate forever. Second, and perhaps even more important, belief in an imminent apocalypse gave comfort and support to the communitarians. The outside world might consider their doctrines odd, even dangerous; the communitarians were usually reviled and often persecuted. But soon, very soon, they thought, all of their sufferings would be justified. Their enemies would be cast down by the returning Christ, and they would stand revealed as the true children of God.

Apocalyptic dreams and millennial hopes have always been close to the hearts of the poor, the persecuted, and the disenchanted. That is why they were so enthusiastically adopted by the Jews, by the early Christians, and by communal groups, right up to the present day.

We don't know when people began to stop considering the Golden Age as a time irrevocably lost, and began to actively prepare for the millennium that was about to dawn. Throughout early Christian history there probably always had been individuals and movements that had attempted to put such plans into practice. But they were minor and they were always crushed by the official Church, which opposed any such radical experiments. The records for the first thousand years of Western Christianity are scanty enough; for losers, they are virtually nonexistent.

Late in the fourteenth century a learned English theologian named John Wycliffe of Oxford was preaching mighty sermons against the worldly excesses of the clergy, as well as launching more subtle attacks on some basic points of Church doctrine. In one of his Latin treatises Wycliffe wrote:

"Firstly, that all good things of God ought to be in common. The proof of this is as follows: Every man ought to be in a state of grace; if he is in a state of grace he is lord of the world and all that it contains; therefore every man ought to be lord of the whole world. But because of the multitudes of men, this will not happen unless they hold all things in common: therefore all things ought to be in common."

Wycliffe himself was no social revolutionary. Attacks on the soft-living, materialistic clergy were commonplace in the fourteenth century. Wycliffe's more radical doctrines, like holding all things in common, were meant as little more than exercises in formal logic. But his teachings inspired less cautious and more desperate men. Among them were a poor preacher named John Ball and a wandering craftsman named Wat Tyler. These two became the leaders of the brief but violent Peasants' Revolt that erupted in England in 1381.

Ball told his ragged followers, "And if we are all descended from one father and one mother, Adam and Eve, how can the lords say or prove that they are more lords than we are—save that they make us dig and till the ground so that they can squander what we produce? . . . Good folk, things cannot go well in England nor ever shall until all things are in common and there is neither villain nor noble, but all of us are of one condition."

The Peasants' Revolt was crushed with much spilling of blood. Tyler was killed, Ball executed, and Wycliffe died just two years later. Though Wycliffe had nothing directly to do with the Peasants' Revolt, his doctrines were deemed heretical and dangerous. Church authorities burned his books and tried to wipe out all traces of the unorthodox scholar. In 1428 they even ordered that his bones be dug up and burned and the ashes thrown into the River Swift. But the spirit of John Wycliffe was not to be exorcised that easily.

At the end of the fourteenth century Wycliffe's reforming doctrines were taken up by a popular Bohemian preacher named John Hus. So effective was Hus's preaching that he frightened both the emperor and the pope. In 1414 Hus was arrested by trickery and burned as a heretic the following year. Still the Hussite movement would not die. The Taborites, the most radical followers of Hus's doctrines, stirred up a string of revolts throughout Bohemia. The Taborites were radical indeed. Not only did they dismiss masses, relics, and images as superstitious nonsense, but they advocated the abolition of the professional priesthood and the abolition of private property and all marks of rank. When these principles were established throughout the world, the Taborites argued that then Christ would descend and the millennium would begin. The Taborite revolts were unsuccessful, but they badly frightened priests, princes, and landowners.

The general religious dissatisfaction was also strong in the German states. There it cast up Martin Luther, a leader who was both more astute and luckier than his predecessors Wycliffe and Hus. However, though Martin Luther sought to overthrow the power of the Roman Catholic Church, he was no social radical. Once Luther gained power, he faithfully supported the interests of the princes who had supported him. When a great revolt broke out among the German peasantry, Luther denounced the rebels with all the fury he had once used to denounce the pope, and he applauded the ultimate massacre of huge numbers of peasants. But Luther was not the only rebel against the established Church. His leading rival in Germany was a preacher named Thomas Muntzer, who not only supported the peasant revolt, but participated in it and was executed for the part he played. Muntzer preached a sort of apocalyptic equalitarianism, and he was to become a hero to many of the later equalitarian movements.

The Lutheran Reformation had some unforeseen but probably inevitable results. When Luther successfully challenged the authority of the Roman Catholic Church, he indirectly brought all worldly authority into disrepute. Luther appealed to the Bible as the sole and final authority in religious matters. Yet once men started reading and interpreting the Bible for themselves, they often came up with interpretations very different from those of Luther. With the structure of the Church removed, people felt that they stood face to face with God and that their only guide was their own conscience. Inevitably some people felt that God spoke directly to them, and what He said ran directly counter to Lutheran as well as Roman Catholic orthodoxy.

Throughout the German-speaking lands there grew a movement called Anabaptism. The name is derived from the practice of baptising adults rather than infants and was first used as an insult. Anabaptism was never a single unified movement; rather it was a loose grouping of forty or so sects, each with its own "divinely inspired" leader. In general the Anabaptists were poor and poorly educated and cared little for theology. To them religion was primarily a matter of inner revelation. Religious forms and rituals were unimportant, and relations between men were to be governed strictly by brotherly love rather than custom, tradition, or law. In many respects the Anabaptists sought to emulate what they held to be the practice of the apostolic church. Most Anabaptists were not communitarians as such, but they respected the ideal of the community of goods and the abolition of private property.

Anabaptist sects tended to be local, exclusive, and highly suspicious of the outside world. Most were strict pacifists who tried to have as little to do with "the world" as possible. They were persecuted, often ferociously, but rarely attempted to strike back against their oppressors. Rather, they retreated more deeply into their own communities, moved when they could, and dreamed of the coming millennium. Usually, when opportunity arose, Anabaptist sects were willing to work hard at establishing good relations with their neighbors.

But not all Anabaptists were pacifists. Around the year 1530 the Anabaptists became very strong in the German city of Munster, and ultimately they were able to take over the town council. Their success attracted Anabaptists from far and wide, most notably two preachers from Holland, Jan Matthys and his young convert Jan Bockelson, who was to become famous under the title of John of Leiden. Matthys and Bockelson soon dominated the town and portrayed Munster as the New Jerusalem, the spot where the millennium would begin. Accordingly they sought to bring about the millennium immediately by, among other things, abolishing private property.

In a pamphlet used as propaganda in other Anabaptist communities they wrote:

"Amongst us God—to whom be eternal praise and thanks —has restored community, as it was in the beginning as befits the saints of God . . . . not only have we put all our belongings into a common pool under the care of deacons, and live from it according to our needs: we praise God through Christ with one heart and mind and are eager to help one another with every kind of service . . . . no Christian or Saint can satisfy God if he does not live in such a community or at least desire with all his heart to live in it."

The reason the Anabaptists of Munster were able to "praise God through Christ with one heart and mind" was that they had expelled from the city all Catholics and Lutherans who would not renounce their faith. They generally proved to be about as intolerant of their opponents as their opponents had been of them. The Anabaptists of Munster soon found themselves under attack by armies hired by the former bishop of the town. On Easter Sunday 1534 Matthys received what he believed to be a divine command to break the siege with a handful of men. He was convinced that with God's aid he and a few followers would be able to drive off the enemy and liberate the town. The small band that set forth was immediately cut to pieces.

Matthys's death opened the way for his young disciple Bockelson, who turned out to be an even more remarkable leader than his master. Through a combination of political astuteness, terroristic policies, and genuine religious fervor, Bockelson induced the town to hold out against a formidable coalition of opponents for well over a year. Had he been a better soldier he might actually have prevailed.

Though the Anabaptist creed had been based on equality, this did not stop Bockelson from setting himself up as king, and no ordinary king either, but as the Messiah of the Last Days. The Anabaptists of Munster had at first regulated sexual behavior very strictly. Adultery was a capital offense. But finding that the women in the city outnumbered the men almost three to one, Bockelson instituted polygamy, becoming perhaps the first leader of a Christian sect to approve the institution. He ultimately had a harem of about fifteen wives. During the long siege the people of Munster were reduced to starvation and utter despair, while Bockelson and his associates went about in magnificent robes and had their comings and goings heralded by the blowing of trumpets. Still, it would be wrong to conclude that Bockelson was a cynical fraud who consciously exploited the people of Munster. Both the leader and his people were living out a powerful fantasy; as ridiculous, even insane, as it seemed to outsiders, it was absolutely real to them.

In the end, of course, the fantasy was shattered. On the night of June 24, 1535, two deserters led the besiegers through the defenses of Munster in a surprise attack. Even then the hopelessly outnumbered Anabaptists fought fiercely, and the few hundred survivors surrendered only after they had been promised safe conduct to their homes.

John of Leiden, shown as king in an engraving believed made
after the fall of Munster.

Almost immediately the bishop's army broke its word, and the survivors were hunted down and exterminated.

Bockelson and two of his leading supporters were publicly tortured to death, but throughout the ordeal the would-be Messiah of the Last Days uttered no sound and made no movement. After the execution the three bodies were put in cages and suspended from a church tower. The cages can be seen in Munster to this day.

The militant Anabaptists tried a few more brief uprisings, but these were all savagely crushed. Militant Anabaptism was dead, but the pacifistic forms survived and heavily influenced both Baptists and Quakers. Theological descendants of the original German Anabaptists under a variety of names—Mennonites, Schwenkfelders, Hutterites, Brethren, and others—were ultimately to migrate to America and form one of the most important parts of American communitarian history.

# 2 ❧ Utopia in the Wilderness

To the Christian nonconformists of the sixteenth and seventeenth centuries, the Old World seemed lost in sin and error. The Protestant reformers were as intolerant as the Catholics of the Inquisition had been, and were often more ruthless at exterminating those who held opposing views. But for the apostolic Christians, indeed for all religious minorities, there seemed a hope almost as bright as the coming of the millennium itself. The hope was the New World, where they could pursue the Christian life as they saw it, free from the harassment of established church or state.

None of the earliest settlers of America tried to live a communal life except briefly and from necessity. Nor was the ideal of religious toleration widespread among the first immigrants. As soon as the Massachusetts Puritans were able, they began persecuting any who did not believe as they did. It was more dangerous to be a Quaker in Massachusetts than in England.

But no single religious group could possibly impose its will on the entire American wilderness—the land was simply too vast and too undeveloped. When Roger Williams objected to the religious intolerance of his Massachusetts neighbors, he moved off to found the colony of Rhode Island. The Quaker William Penn acquired vast tracts of land in what is now Pennsylvania, and that colony became a haven for sects even more unpopular than the Quakers themselves. No sect, no matter how odd its doctrines or how despised it had been in Europe, was without hope of finding refuge in the American wilderness.

The first communitarians to arrive were followers of the doctrines preached by Jean de Labadié. By advocating a communal way of life, de Labadié had attracted some supporters and many enemies in Europe. The Labadists had been forced to wander from place to place until, at the end of the seventeenth century, they came to rest in Holland under the protection of a powerful lord, whose daughter had joined the group. In Holland the Labadists prospered and began looking toward establishing a colony in the New World. The Labadists were first persuaded to go to Surinam, in South America, the only remaining Dutch colony in the New World. But they soon found that the attractions of Surinam had been badly misrepresented to them. Rather than being a land of milk and honey, Surinam was hot and disease ridden, and they were glad to leave it as soon as they could. The Labadists next purchased a tract of land called Bohemia Manor in Maryland, near the Pennsylvania border, and proceeded to set up a community that at its height included over one hundred men, women, and children.

The Labadists were frugal and hardworking, and the community had excellent prospects for success. But it soon fell under the domination of one of its energetic but unscrupulous members, Peter Sluyter. Though Sluyter imposed rules of rigorous austerity on the members of his group, he was not very strict about obeying the rules himself. Labadist doctrine found slavery abhorrent, but Sluyter became a notorious slaveowner. Finally he had the colony members divide up their communal land under private ownership, with Sluyter himself getting the largest portion of the property. When Peter Sluyter died in 1722, he was a rich man, but the group he had led was a failure. Within a few years after the death of Sluyter the colony had disbanded. What its fate might have been under more honest leadership is not possible to say.

The next communal group to establish itself in America was genuinely exotic. Among the many deeply religious Germans who had become disenchanted with the direction the Reformation had taken was an ex-Lutheran preacher named Johann Jacob Zimmermann. In some respects Zimmermann was what we would today call a fundamentalist, a believer in literal interpretation of the Bible. But, in addition to his biblical fundamentalism, he was an enthusiastic astrologer and a believer in a variety of mystical doctrines. By combining biblical interpretation and astrological calculation Zimmermann had concluded that the world was going to end in the autumn of 1694. The problem of how and where to greet the returning Christ has always perplexed sincere apocalyptists. Zimmermann believed that he had found his answer in the Book of Revelation. There it was written that the true church, symbolized by a woman, was given "two wings of a great eagle, that she might fly into the wilderness, into her place, where she is nourished for a time, and times, and half a time, from the face of the serpent." Thus it seemed clear to Zimmermann that the place to usher in the end of the world was the virgin wilderness of America.

The day before Zimmermann and his little band of followers were to set sail for the New World, the prophet died. Leadership was assumed by Zimmermann's strange but immensely learned young follower Johannes Kelpius. To Zimmermann's fundamentalism, astrology, and mysticism

*Cloister of the Seventh Day Baptists at Ephrata, Pennsylvania.*

Kelpius added his own interest in such esoteric doctrines as alchemy, Rosicrucianism, and a good deal of ancient German superstition to boot.

After a voyage in which they believed that they had been miraculously saved at least twice, the little brotherhood landed at Chesapeake Bay on June 19, 1694. They made their way inland and settled briefly among the German colonists in Pennsylvania. Despite the oddness of their ideas Kelpius and his associates were popular with the more conventional settlers. They hoped that the well-educated band of brothers would serve as teachers for the community. It was with considerable disappointment that the settlers watched the brethren march off to an isolated spot in the wilderness on which they built their tabernacle where they were to await the end of the world.

The wooden tabernacle constructed by the brethren was forty feet square and contained forty cells for the forty members; forty obviously was a number of mystical significance to the group. Kelpius, who was even more of a hermit than his associates, retired to a cave nearby. The community came to be known as The Woman in the Wilderness—that is, the church in the wilderness.

The brethren of The Woman in the Wilderness were celibate, ascetic, and practiced total communal ownership of goods. For a while the community's obsession with the presumed end of the world kept things running smoothly. They had little time to fret over earthly matters, and they spent many hours seated on the roof of their tabernacle taking turns staring through a telescope to see if they could discern any signs of the approaching end in the sky.

The end first predicted by Zimmermann, the fall of 1694, passed practically before the community got started. This, however, discouraged them only slightly. It is difficult for outsiders to understand or believe how often a confirmed millennialist can be disappointed without his faith being shaken in the least. Time after time the brethren thought that they had seen unmistakable signs of the approaching end, only to have them come to nothing. One night a glowing form that seemed to be an angel appeared before them. They fell to their knees and awaited the announcement of Judgement Day, but the glowing form said nothing and soon faded away. Three days later the same thing happened. And still they waited confidently for their predictions to be fulfilled.

While waiting, the brethren were busy, and they did not cut themselves off entirely from the world. They were compulsive educators, and to spread their gospel they took up printing. Music was the only real relaxation that the ascetic brethren allowed themselves, and Kelpius seems to have been a particularly keen musician. The first book of music printed in America was probably printed at The Woman in the Wilderness. Under the mistaken, but common, belief that American Indians were the descendants of the Ten Lost Tribes of Israel, the brethren were extremely anxious to establish good relations with the Indians and to evangelize them. To this end they compiled an invaluable vocabulary of Indian words.

After some years, however, the endless cycle of rising hope and severe disappointment about the return of Christ finally wore down the brethren, and the community began to break up. The first to depart were the best educated and most active. Kelpius himself clung stubbornly to the belief that the millennium would arrive within his lifetime and that he consequently would never die. He continually expressed this belief though he was dying of tuberculosis, his condition made worse by fasting and austerity. Kelpius assured his followers that he was merely suffering from a series of "heavy colds." Only when his death was imminent and absolutely certain did Johannes Kelpius come to doubt the millennial doctrines that had brought him to the American wilderness. Kelpius died at the age of thirty-five, and was buried by his stunned followers near the tabernacle in which they had all expected to greet the returning Christ. With his death the community of The Woman in the Wilderness also effectively died, though a few members hung on in the region for nearly forty more years. The remaining brethren lived primarily as ascetic hermits whose sole purpose in life seemed to be preparing for their own death.

In 1720 another group of German religious mystics came to the New World with the intention of joining the brethren at The Woman in the Wilderness. But when they arrived, they found the community virtually extinct, so they moved on to other German communities in the region. Among the immigrants was a baker's son named Johann Conrad Beis-

*A sleeping cell at the Ephrata cloister.*

sel. He was a member of a sect known as the Seventh Day Baptists. They practiced adult baptism and observed the Sabbath on Saturday rather than Sunday.

Beissel was a small, intense man with a magnetic speaking voice and apparently an excellent talent for organization. He gathered a group of followers from among the German immigrants and began a communal settlement in Pennsylvania in a place he called Ephrata, an alternate name for Bethlehem. Today the remains of the Ephrata community, magnificently restored, are a popular tourist attraction in Pennsylvania's Lancaster County. The Ephrata restoration can give the visitor a unique look at what life must have been like in this early American community, and the picture is a grim one indeed.

From the outside, the big wooden buildings with their narrow windows look foreboding, even in the parklike setting provided by the restorers. Inside, the impression is not merely one of austerity, but of deliberate mortification of the flesh. Seated on one of the benches in the chapel, the visitor soon discovers that not only is one forced to sit up straight, but that it is absolutely impossible to find a comfortable position. Yet it was on these benches that the Ephratians were obliged to sit through Beissel's interminable sermons and Bible readings. Also, all the passageways and doors in the buildings are too narrow and low for an ordinary person to walk through without bending. This was a constant reminder that "narrow is the way that leadeth unto life."

The most depressing impression is made by the individual cells in which the members of the community slept. These were a mere six feet by seven feet by nine feet in height. Such luxuries as a mattress were regarded with scorn. The bed itself scarcely deserves the name, for it was a narrow plank of wood, with a block of wood in place of a pillow.

In the original buildings of Ephrata practically everything was made of wood, including the hinges on the doors. Even the plates off which the community members took their meals and the vessels from which they drank were originally of wood. The use of metal for shaping and working wood was shunned. One writer has suggested that the dimensions of the buildings were based on the supposed dimensions of Solomon's Temple, and that the prohibition on metal tools was inspired by the biblical description of the construction of the Temple where "there was neither hammer, nor axe, nor any tool of iron, heard in the house while it was in building." This prohibition of metal seems to have been relaxed in later years, for there is much metal to be seen in the restored buildings, some of it dating to Beissel's time.

This austere community naturally was celibate. Women were admitted, but a strict segregation of the sexes was maintained. The Spiritual Virgins, as the sisters of the order were called, originally had their quarters on the top floor of the community's first building. But as the order grew, they were given their own separate building.

Both brothers and sisters dressed alike in coarse woolen habits, which were intolerably hot and uncomfortable in the summer; and both went barefoot at all times, which was intolerably cold and uncomfortable in the winter. The women cut their hair short, while the men were tonsured like monks and wore full beards, of which they seemed very proud.

The daily routine at Ephrata was grim and joyless, in keeping with the architecture and clothing. The community members went to bed at nine, only to be roused by a bell rung at midnight by Beissel himself. They trooped to the chapel for an hour of services and then went back to bed until five, when another bell signaled them to another hour of services. At six they began work, and this went on until nine, when they finally had breakfast. Breakfast, like most meals at Ephrata, was meager to the point of malnutrition. It consisted of thin gruel and dry bread. Those who visited the community often noted that the members looked dangerously thin. Meals were eaten in silence, except for Bible

*Interior of the chapel at the Ephrata cloister.*

reading at the beginning and end. Somehow this inadequate fare managed to sustain the Ephratians and give them enough strength for the most severe physical labors. Customarily the brothers themselves pulled the carts and carried the loads, tasks usually performed by mules and horses. The workday ended at six, and after supper the Ephratians were allowed to spend two hours studying and writing before they went to bed.

One of the things that they wrote was a weekly report confessing all sins committed or contemplated. These reports were read aloud by Beissel at services, and were discussed and criticized by the community as a whole.

Life in the Ephrata cloister sounds unbearably severe. But often such routines seem worse when written out than when actually observed, for, in practice, rules are frequently bent and broken.

Although the celibate orders formed the nucleus of Ephrata, much of its strength came from the lay members, families who helped to support the community and who often lived in the vicinity. These household members, as they were called, not only avoided celibacy, but also enjoyed such luxuries as mattresses and shoes. When lay members wished to lead a more rigorous religious life, they could join one of the celibate orders; if that routine proved too difficult, they could always return to their families, and not be entirely separated from the community.

As with the brethren of The Woman in the Wilderness, music was a great joy to the Ephratians. The choir of Spiritual Virgins was renowned for its singing. Beissel and a few other members of the community were also writers, and they either printed themselves or had printed by outsiders (including Benjamin Franklin) books that they wrote or that otherwise interested them. Both brothers and sisters were adept at making illuminated manuscripts and wall hangings. The Ephratians were, in general, far better educated than their neighbors and were much sought after as

teachers. Indeed, the school established by the Ephrata
brethren ultimately became more important than the community itself.

At the core of the entire Ephrata experiment was Conrad
Beissel—the founder, leader, preacher, and inspiration for
the community. The people called him Father Friedsam
Gottrecht. Beissel was a man of enormous energy, strength,
and tenacity, and not for one minute did he ever doubt his
own abilities or the righteousness of his cause. Some of his
disaffected followers and other opponents accused Beissel
of behaving as if he were a second Christ, and although the
charge is not really accurate, it is not without foundation
either. Beissel believed himself to be directly inspired by
God, and anyone who disagreed with him, even slightly, was
denounced as a sinner, and expelled from the community if
he did not submit completely to Father Friedsam's will.

The problem presented by a man like Conrad Beissel is
one that occurs again and again in the history of communes.
The communes were based on the principle of equalitarianism; yet they were usually under the domination of a single
strong individual. Though the leader was often a very benevolent despot, he or she was a despot nonetheless.

Other, and more serious, charges were leveled against
Beissel. One was that he was a swindler who, like Sluyter at
Bohemia Manor, got rich at the expense of his starving and
deluded followers. A visit to Ephrata today indicates that
Beissel did live better than the brethren and sisters. He had
his own cottage, with a large stove for warming himself and
for baking bread. He could, if he desired, take his meals
alone, rather than in the cold communal dining room. But
his bed and pillow were a narrow plank and a block of wood
like those used by the others. Although his community
prospered, it might have become wealthy had Beissel
not continually turned down opportunities to increase
Ephrata's wealth on the theory (almost certainly correct)
that extra wealth would have been bad for the spiritual

purity of the group. Because of this, the charge that Conrad Beissel was a religious swindler will not stick.

Communes, particularly those as curious as Beissel's, rarely make their neighbors very comfortable. Almost inevitably stories of strange activities will be spread. At Ephrata the stories centered on Beissel's alleged special interest in the Spiritual Virgins. These suspicions about Beissel may not have been complete fabrications; although there is certainly no evidence to prove that Father Friedsam ever broke his vow of celibacy, he did seem to take particular pleasure in the company of women. Neighbors unsympathetic to Ephrata pictured him as a fiend who held lewd orgies in the woods near the cloister. There was even a short-lived plot to burn the community down, but it came to nothing. Neighbors grumbled and gossiped, but finally accepted Ephrata.

By 1678, when Beissel died, Ephrata was flourishing. Many of those who had once objected to the community vied to get their children into its school. A few branches of the community were even set up at other places, but they never amounted to much.

Although Ephrata stopped growing after Beissel's death, it didn't die. There were still a few hundred Ephratians (called Seventh Day German Baptists) in America during the first few decades of this century. However, the celibate orders had long since disappeared, and as early as 1786 the members had abandoned their communal life. Still, Ephrata represents one of the longest-lived and most successful communal experiments in American history.

# 3 🌿 The Shakers

The long Shaker adventure is finally drawing to a close. The society, which at its height had over six thousand members scattered throughout eighteen communities, has now been reduced to a handful of elderly sisters living in two New England villages. There has been occasional talk of trying to revive the society, but there is no spirit behind the talk. The truth is that the Shakers have been dying for a hundred years. The wonder is that they lasted so long—indeed that they existed at all.

"We feel it is time to close this adventure," said Sister Bertha, one of the elderly Shakeresses at the Canterbury, New Hampshire, settlement. "Mother Ann Lee, our founder, prophesied that we would one day dwindle until there were not enough of us left to bury our dead. The good we have done will not be lost. Someone will pick up the way."

The Shakers did not always have such a modest appraisal of their place in history. The full and correct title of the group is The United Society of Believers in Christ's Second Appearing. When the Shakers wrote up their bylaws, they called them Millennial Laws. Their poems were collected into a volume called *Millennial Praises*. The Shakers were not only confirmed millennialists, but also believed that the millennium had begun with them and that their founder was a second Christ. To the Shakers, however, the dawning of the millennium was no single apocalyptic event; it was a very personal experience. The millennium that had been prophesied so often came to each individual who joined the order and accepted its strict rules of behavior.

The religious heritage of the Shakers goes back to a sect of radical Protestants called the French Prophets who fled their native land at the end of the seventeenth century. A few of the exiled Prophets settled in England, and though they were free to preach, they never gathered much of a following. Their most lasting influence was upon James and Jane Wardley, a Quaker tailor and his wife, from the city of Manchester. In about 1747 the Wardleys quit the Society of Friends to start their own sect, based upon the teachings of the French.

Neither the French Prophets nor their English disciples had an organized theology. Like the Quakers, they laid heavy stress on individual inspiration. But while Quaker meetings were becoming more quiet and respectable, the Wardleys' meetings were going in the other direction, becoming more noisy and even violent. A later Shaker history described these meetings: "At other times they were affected, under the power of God, with a mighty shaking; and were occasionally exercised in singing, shouting, or walking the floor, under the influence of spiritual signs, shoving each other about. . . ." These energetic religious activities earned the Wardley followers the title of Shaking Quakers and, ultimately, Shakers, a name they adopted with pride.

The Wardleys' most notable convert, though it didn't seem so at the time, was a plump, illiterate twenty-two-year-old working girl named Ann Lee (or Lees). At first Ann did not play a very active part in the sect, but as her personal troubles accumulated, she turned more and more for comfort

*Shakers dancing as part of their worship service.*

and escape to the emotional religion she found at the Wardleys' home.

Ann Lee's troubles began with her marriage in 1762 to Abraham Standerin, a Manchester blacksmith. Since she had been a little girl, Ann had been disgusted by the thought of sex. She had no desire to get married at all, and did so only at the strong urging of her parents. Over the next few years she bore four children, all of whom died in infancy. During her last pregnancy Ann herself very nearly died.

According to official Shaker histories, these experiences strengthened Ann's conviction that sex lay at the core of man's sinfulness. The deaths of her children were her proof of God's displeasure and punishment. She avoided her husband's bed "as if it had been made of embers." She fasted and prayed until she became so weak that she could not stand. Finally she experienced what she believed to be a spiritual rebirth: "My soul broke forth to God."

During her ordeal the Wardleys had been a great source of support, and after she regained her health, Ann began to take a more active part in the sect. Her views on sex and marriage came to be adopted by the Wardleys and their small band of followers.

The Shaker group gained some new converts, including Ann's father and younger brother William, both of whom had been previously opposed to the Wardleys' doctrines. Though still a tiny sect, the Shakers grew bolder in their preaching and worship. Their denunciations of the sins of the world were stronger, and their meetings louder and longer, often continuing well into the night. They were widely disliked, and because of the strangeness and rowdiness of their activities, not a little feared. Mobs regularly broke up Shaker meetings, and Ann Lee herself was often beaten and stoned. Each time she survived one of these attacks she attributed it to divine intervention on her behalf, and every new torment only fortified her faith.

The police also interrupted Shaker meetings for a variety of reasons; Sabbath breaking was the most common. The usual result was a small fine or short jail sentence for the Shakers, but in 1773 Ann Lee received an extended sentence of approximately thirty days. In future years Ann often repeated the horrors inflicted upon her during this period of imprisonment. Though much of what she said is probably untrue, she may well have believed her own stories and the rest of the Shakers certainly did. It was during this imprisonment, say Shaker historians, that Ann Lee had the "grand vision of the very transgression of the first man and woman in the Garden of Eden, the cause wherein all mankind was lost and separated from God." Christ then appeared to her in the vision and told her that it was her mission to go forth and preach the celibate life. In describing the vision she said, "I have been walking in fine valleys with Christ, as with a lover . . . ."

When she emerged from prison, Ann told her followers, "I am Ann of the Word." She displaced the Wardleys as Shaker leaders by boldly announcing that Jane Wardley was "John the Baptist in the female line"; the meaning was clear—she, Ann Lee, was Christ in the female line. Ann Lee adopted the title of "Mother" or "Mother of the New Creation."

Mother Ann's doctrine was a simple one: All of the world's ills from disease to war to the inequality of the sexes were the result of concupiscence, or sexual desire. The only way to achieve salvation was to abandon sex entirely. The Shakers had only one other rule, public oral confession of all sins.

At this critical point of her career Ann Lee was in her middle thirties. She was short, rather stout, with brown hair and "penetrating" blue eyes. Modern psychologists might have a good deal to say about her hysterical aversion to sex, but there is no simple explanation for the absolute devotion she could inspire in her followers. Whatever Ann Lee may have been, she was neither the charlatan nor the madwoman that her enemies said she was.

For the months following Ann Lee's release from prison the Shakers were left alone by the police and the mobs, but Shakerism gained no new converts. In fact, many of the older members, including the now displaced Wardleys, seem to have drifted away. In the spring of 1774 Mother Ann had a series of visions indicating that the sect should migrate to America. This vision was inspired by the same passage from the Book of Revelation that had moved the brethren of The Woman in the Wilderness to America.

The news of the planned emigration was received joyously by the Shakers, but when the time came to move, only eight of the congregation, including Mother Ann, her brother James, her niece Nancy, and odd as it may seem, her husband, Abraham Standerin, boarded the ship *Mariah* for the passage to the New World. Standerin's reasons for

*Retiring room, or bedroom, of an early Shaker member.*

making the trip can only be guessed at, for he was never a Shaker nor did he have any sympathy for his wife's ideas.

According to Shaker legend, the ship bearing the little party nearly sank, but was saved by a miracle after Mother Ann had a vision in which an angel promised them safety.

The Shaker band arrived at New York harbor on August 6, 1774. They had little money and no real plans for the future. Their course of action was, as always, simply to wait for divine inspiration. In the meantime, the Shakers drifted off to seek employment for themselves wherever they could. Mother Ann worked as a domestic, and her husband, the enigmatic Standerin, was employed in a smithy. The pair may even have lived together, at least during a period when Standerin was ill. Mother Ann's powers of persuasion never had any effect upon her husband. When he was well, he began to frequent taverns, and one night he brought a prostitute home and threatened to marry her unless Mother Ann renounced her vow of celibacy. This apparently was too much for Mother Ann—sometime during the year of 1775 the prophetess severed her marriage bond.

The founding of a community was not basic to Shaker belief, but they did want a permanent base of operations, from which they could preach their gospel without interference. Some of the members purchased a tract of land called Niskeyuna (later called Watervliet) near Albany, New York. It was poor swampy land, in the middle of what was then virgin wilderness. This was an odd place from which to start what they hoped would be a worldwide movement, but it was all the Shakers could afford. Mother Ann herself did not join the community until 1776, the year the American Revolution began.

The physical hardships of life in the wilderness were bearable. The Shakers had never been rich and were accustomed to hardship. For Ann Lee the life of a prophetess in the wilderness was certainly preferable to that of a laundress in New York City. More difficult to bear, and to understand,

*Communal kitchen in an early Shaker settlement.*

was the total lack of interest that Americans displayed in the Shaker faith. Between 1776 and 1780 the society gained only one American convert despite all their efforts. But Mother Ann went right on predicting that soon a great multitude would come together at Niskeyuna.

Religious revivals—some of them quite hysterical—had been a regular feature of the American scene since 1734. In mid-1779 one of these excitements broke out among a group called the New Light Baptists centered in the vicinity of New Lebanon, New York. For months the New Lights held nightly meetings in which members of the congregation screamed, shouted, fainted, and had visions. All of the preaching and all of the visions pointed to one thing— Judgement Day was coming very soon. But as winter began and Judgement Day had not yet arrived, the revival fervor abated, leaving many of the New Lights exhausted and disappointed.

*Communal dining room in an early Shaker settlement.*

Early the following spring, two disillusioned New Lights were heading westward to make a new life for themselves when they, by chance, came across the Shaker settlement. The Shakers told them that the Judgement Day, for which they had waited in vain the previous year, was taking place that very moment at Niskeyuna. Judgement Day came to all who confessed their sins and entered the celibate life of the spirit. For such individuals, the world that they had known was at an end, and they were saved for all eternity. This doctrine was strange and revolutionary, but very appealing to the unhappy millennialists. The community at Niskeyuna appeared to possess the sort of religious purity that the New Lights had been seeking. Instead of proceeding westward, the travelers went back to New Lebanon to tell others what they had found.

Another New Light was delegated to visit the Shakers. He too returned home puzzled, but very nearly convinced that this obscure sect, headed by a woman, did indeed represent the long awaited Coming. The woman leader had particularly bothered the New Lights, who believed with Saint Paul that women should "keep silence in the Churches." Mother Ann explained her idea of the family of Christ having both a male and female line. "He is the Father and she the Mother; and all the children, both male and female, must be subject to their parents; and the woman, being second, must be subject to her husband, who is the first; but when the man is gone, the right of government belongs to the woman."

Although the New Lights had some trouble with the strange Shaker theology, they had little trouble with the rule of celibacy. A segment of Christianity had always regarded celibacy as a superior spiritual state. Marriage was tolerated only because it was better than fornication. The Puritan tradition that was strong in America at that time was particularly concerned with the conflict of the spirit and the flesh. Rather than being an obstacle to making further converts, celibacy in the early days of Shakerism was one of its great attractions.

Among the first converts in 1780 was Joseph Meacham, a lay preacher and one of the leaders of the New Lebanon Revival. Meacham, a tall, austere New England farmer with a genius for organization, was to become, next to Mother Ann herself, the most important figure in Shaker history.

The flood of new converts Mother Ann had confidently predicted never really arrived, but large numbers did attend the public "testimonies" at Niskeyuna, and some joined the sect. This brought the Shakers to the attention of the New York authorities, who had previously been unaware of their existence. To the authorities the Shakers seemed an unsavory lot, for not only did they preach pacifism during wartime, but they also were recent immigrants from Britain. With a war against Britain going on, the Shakers were strongly suspected of pro-British sympathies. Some of the

*A group of Shakers, Mt. Lebanon, New York, in typical dress.*

Shaker leaders, including Mother Ann, were imprisoned in Albany and Poughkeepsie. But the imprisonment brought both publicity and sympathy for the order. It soon became clear that the Shakers were not pro-British nor politically dangerous in any other way. They had come to America to practice their religious beliefs freely; to imprison them seemed a betrayal of the very principles for which the revolution was being fought. The Shaker leaders were released

*The ring dance, one of the ritualistic dances performed during
early Shaker worship services.*

and allowed to preach their doctrines without interference
from the state government.

Mother Ann's little flock had grown considerably during
1780, and by spring of the following year they were determined to actively spread the word throughout the New
England states. Thus began one of the most violent, yet vital
phases of Shaker history. The Shakers were not received joyously by all they visited. None of the conventional churches
were happy to entertain these rival preachers with their
strange doctrines. Shaker celibacy and confession of sins
reminded many Protestants of the Catholic church, which
they detested. It was rumored that the Shakers preached
celibacy in order to sap the strength of the new nation. Besides, early Shaker worship was wild and could easily shock
or frighten more staid observers. One unfriendly contemporary described a Shaker service this way:

"When they meet together for their worship, they fall

a-groaning and trembling, and every one acts alone for himself; one will fall prostrate on the floor, another on his knees and his head in his hands; another will be muttering articulate sounds, which neither they or any body else understand. Some will be singing, each one his own tune; some without words, in an Indian tune, some sing jig tunes, some tunes of their own meaning, in an unknown mutter, which they call new tongues; some will be dancing, and others stand laughing, heartily and loudly . . . others will be agonizing, as though they were in great pain; others jumping up and down; others fluttering over somebody, and talking to them; others will be shooing and hissing evil spirits out of the house, till the different tunes . . . makes a perfect bedlam; this they call the worship of God."

Yet it would be quite wrong to think that the Shakers faced a land made up entirely of rigid and unemotional Puritans. We have already mentioned the revival among the New Light Baptists that contributed to the early growth of the Shakers. Another sect that provided many new converts for the Shakers was the Free Will Baptists, whose services became so energetic they earned themselves the nickname of "Merry Dancers."

When the Shakers moved to the town of Harvard, Massachusetts, they occupied an odd, square-roofed house that had been built as a refuge by a preacher named Shadrack Ireland. Ireland had proclaimed himself the New Messiah and had prophesied the coming of the millennium. He claimed that if he ever died he would rise again in three days. His followers kept watch over his body for three weeks, before they finally gave up on his resurrection and buried him in a cornfield.

So it was into a society that offered both hostility and great potential that the Shakers extended their mission. As in England, American Shaker meetings were often broken up by gangs, and Mother Ann particularly was the target of stonings and beatings. On more than one occasion, she

*A sawmill, one of the many types of mills at Pleasant
Hill, Kentucky.*

was dragged brutally through the streets, before being rescued. Stories that Shakers regularly attended their meetings drunk and that sometimes all the participants stripped naked were widely circulated and helped to incite the mobs. There were even hints of witchcraft at Shaker rites.

For the Shakers the benefits of their mission to New England far outweighed the hardships. They made many converts, including some prosperous farmers whose lands were donated to the society and became the centers for future Shaker settlements.

It was necessity, rather than planning, that made the Shakers adopt a communal way of life. Though they made occasional references to the Book of Acts and to the presumed life of the apostolic church, Shaker communism grew in a haphazard way in the early years. The Shakers found that with their ideas they could not easily live in regular society. Thus the idea of building separate Shaker communities started shortly after the group came to America. At first many converts continued to live outside of these centers. The common ownership of all goods was another natural outgrowth of Shaker life. As celibates, they had no family to provide for, and they were required by their beliefs to live simply, so there was nothing on which they could spend any accumulated wealth. By about 1783 Shakers were being strongly encouraged by their leaders to "sell their possessions and give to the poor."

Unlike Shadrack Ireland and so many other would-be messiahs, Mother Ann never preached that she would live forever or rise from the dead. On the contrary, Shaker doctrine strongly rejected the idea of physical immortality and resurrection of the body as both absurd and unnecessary. Still, when Mother Ann died at Niskeyuna on September 8, 1784, it came as a great shock to her followers. They had persuaded themselves that somehow she would always be there to guide them, and when she died, there was a wave of disillusionment and many resigned from the society.

Leadership fell to Father James Whittaker, one of those who had accompanied Mother Ann from England. Whittaker's parents had become Shakers so he was introduced to the sect while still a boy, and knew no other life. Father James was in his early thirties when he became supreme leader of the Shakers. He was a powerful preacher and so zealous in his defense of the Shaker way of life that many called him a fanatic. Some of the leading Shakers despised him.

Father James made the shrewd decision that it was a waste of energy and resources to continue to attempt mass conversions. He thought it better to concentrate on consolidating the gains already made. He traveled incessantly between the various Shaker societies, encouraging, exhorting, and admonishing them to continue the task set forth by Mother Ann. But in July of 1787, Father James Whittaker died, at only thirty-six years of age.

Father James' death was a moment of extreme crisis for the Shakers. The two principal leaders had died before the society had become firmly established. The Shakers could easily have gone the way of The Woman in the Wilderness and a thousand other sects that have sprung up throughout history, only to dissolve after the death of the founders. But the quality of people attracted to Shakerism was unusually high, and at this critical moment the movement found two leaders who fitted its needs perfectly.

The Shakers were "inspired" to appoint as their new supreme leader Joseph Meacham, one of the earliest American converts from the New Light revival. One of Meacham's first official acts was to appoint another remarkable individual, Lucy Wright, to lead "in the female line." Both of these people had been well known to Mother Ann, and she had fully appreciated their qualities. She had called Father Joseph "the wisest man that has been born of a woman for six hundred years." Upon the conversion of Lucy Wright, she said that gaining her was "equal to gaining a nation."

*A typical Shaker meetinghouse at Mt. Lebanon, New York. The building still stands today.*

Father Joseph immediately set about establishing a firm organizational basis for the society. All Shakers who still lived outside of Shaker communities were strongly encouraged to join a community. Each community, or society, was subdivided into families—an ironic name for an order of confirmed celibates. Each family was led by two elders and two elderesses whose duty it was to see to the spiritual and temporal needs of all family members. Authority among the Shakers was, in Father Joseph's words, "from the head to the toe." The leaders appointed their own subordinates and successors. Although in theory any member might speak out when the spirit moved him, in practice there was no appeal from the decisions of the elders and elderesses. Yet, in general, the leaders seem to have been a benevolent and efficient group, and the Shakers were rarely torn by the sort of fierce internal struggles that afflicted many communal societies.

*Interior of the meetinghouse at Mt. Lebanon.*

Under Father Joseph the Shakers tried to minimize their conflict with the rest of the world. Denunciations of the sinfulness of others were toned down, and the Shakers set about trying to gain converts by example, rather than by terrifying them with tales of eternal damnation.

Father Joseph lived only until 1791, and then absolute leadership passed into the hands of Mother Lucy, who guided the society until her death in 1821.

Although a communal form of life had been more or less implied in early Shaker organizations, Father Joseph was very specific on this point:

"All the members of the Church have a just and equal right to the use of things, according to their order and needs; no other difference ought to be made, between the Elder or younger in things spiritual or temporal, than that which is just, and is for the peace and unity, and good of the whole."

*Shaker women labeling and wrapping the bottles containing the Shaker extract of roots, sold as a general remedy.*

Once the Shakers were an economic community, joining was no longer merely a matter of confessing sins and living a celibate life. All who wished to join had to be free from outside debts and obligations. Mother Ann had insisted upon this, and under Father Joseph and his successors, the rule was strictly enforced. Those who wished to join went through a long trial period, usually a year, during which they were free to leave at any time, with whatever they had put into the society restored to them. Even those who became full-fledged Shakers and later desired to leave were given some sort of cash settlement to pay for the work that they had done while members. The number of ex-Shakers who felt cheated by such settlements was surprisingly small, and if the apostates took their cases to court, the judgements were almost invariably in favor of the Shakers.

The Shakers never engaged in social or political activity, but the humanitarian ideas that they professed and practiced were far in advance of those held by most religious groups of their day, or of the present day for that matter. They were committed pacifists. Shaker brothers who had served in the army before joining the order even refused to collect their pensions.

To the Shakers, slavery was one of the worst human evils. Not only did they refuse to own slaves or to benefit in any way from slave labor, but membership in the society was open to slaves and to Indians. A lot of antislavery churches of the time talked about all men being brothers, but few opened their doors to blacks and Indians.

Equality of the sexes was a basic doctrine of the order, hardly a surprising one, since the founder was a woman. Even after Mother Ann's death, however, women continued to be important in running the society. The sisters of the society did all the traditional women's work—sewing, cooking, and so forth—while the men did most of the farming and heavy labor. But the work of the sisters was in no way considered inferior, and in the later days of the Shakers it was the sisters who kept the society going.

An unusual feature of Shaker life was that they preached kindness to animals. Most Shakers became vegetarians, and ultimately the order abandoned its once-profitable stock raising business.

The Shakers were always charitable. No hungry person was turned away without a meal, and the Shakers dispensed huge quantities of clothes and tools for the needy. One cynical explanation for the growth of the Shaker movement was that they provided free food and clothes to all comers. The society acknowledged some problem with "winter Shakers," those who joined because they had no place to go during the colder months. But once in the order there was no charity; everyone worked. All observers agreed that those who did not positively love to work felt uncomfortable among the Shakers and soon left.

Next to their celibacy, the most notable feature of Shaker

life was the care that they took with their work. The intimate relationship between work and worship went back to Mother Ann; her phrase was "put your hands to work, and your hearts to God." Mother Ann and the early English Shakers had come from the urban working class. The early American converts were primarily farmers, artisans, and craftsmen. They were largely practical New Englanders, raised in the Puritan tradition where work and worship were one in the same. The accumulation of wealth was not the object of hard work; the job well done was itself sufficient reward.

All activities in the society were to be ruled by the principles of "order and use." Says Shaker doctrine:

"All work done, or things made in the Church for their own use ought to be faithfully, and well done, but plain and without superfluity. All things ought to be made according to their order and use; and all things kept decent and in good order, according to their order and use. All things made for sale ought to be well done, and suitable for their use. . . .

"All ought to dress in plain and modest apparel, but clean and decent according to their order and calling, and suitable to their employ, and to the season and state of the weather, neither too high nor too low, but in a just and temperate medium, suitable for example to others."

Although the Shakers professed to hate "the flesh," they also took exceptionally good care of it. The early Shakers had been accused of sleeping on chains and practicing other mortifications of the flesh, but such practices, if indeed they had ever existed, soon disappeared. Luxury was abhorrent to the Shakers, but comfort certainly was not. So comfortable did they become that one observer of Shaker societies

OPPOSITE: *Shaker sisters and brother, Dr. Francis Pennebaker, the village dentist, on the steps of a family house at Pleasant Hill, Kentucky.*

felt that the renunciation of marriage was "the sum of Shaker asceticism."

Among the Shakers there was no sleeping on wooden planks or going about barefoot in the winter as there had been at Ephrata. Despite their real love of work, the Shakers were always careful never to drive themselves too hard. Work was to be a pleasure, not a punishment. They never worked at a single task too long—a farmer one day would be a blacksmith the next. Theirs was not the most efficient method of dividing up labor, but it helped to keep up interest in the work.

Even when the Shakers were most numerous, they were always obliged to hire outside help on their farms and in their workshops. Most observers noticed that the hired help usually worked faster and harder than did the Shakers themselves. But the Shakers were always popular employers, for they paid well and were known for their fairness and kindliness toward their employees.

Sickness was a sin to the Shakers, so they tried very hard to avoid getting sick. They were meticulously, almost fanatically, clean. They took great care in what they ate—today they might be classed as health food nuts. Buildings were well and evenly heated. It can't be said with any certainty that the Shakers were healthier than the general run of the population, but the records do indicate that a significantly large number of them lived well into their seventies and beyond. Certainly the Shakers seem to have lived more comfortably than most of "the world's" people at that time.

Still it was the practice of celibacy that excited and still excites the most interest. Over and over again the question is asked, "What would have happened to the human race if everybody had become a Shaker?" Most people find something monstrously illogical, if not downright wicked, in a sect whose ultimate aim appears to have been the extinction of the human race.

The Shakers tried to respond to this objection in a pamphlet first printed in 1868 and reprinted many times thereafter. They claimed that they did not condemn marriage entirely, nor did they consider procreation a great wrong. According to the pamphlet, "the great Architect has divers grades of workmen, all necessary in their places . . . to complete the building." Even in nature, the Shakers asserted, millions of seeds never germinated. "Nature designed vastly the greater proportion of vegetable seeds for the support of animal life, and thus to pass into a higher grade of being, at the expense and destruction of their use for reproduction." Thomas Malthus, whose theories of overpopulation were popular at the time, was then appealed to, and the Shakers pictured themselves as part of a system of checks and balances on overpopulation.

Somehow, the argument doesn't carry conviction. One suspects that the original Shakers were untroubled by the vision of the extinction of the human race. Men and women of the flesh were lost in sin and wickedness anyhow. By their philosophy, if the whole world became Shaker, then the whole world would be saved, the hated flesh would no longer be needed, and the spirits of all mankind would live in glory forever with the Lord. This position is neither unusual nor heartless, for other Christian millennialists hoped devoutly for the fiery end of this world and the dawning of a newer and brighter world.

In practice the maintenance of celibacy became highly ritualized. Despite persistent rumors of orgies and perversions, and though the sexes in Shaker communities lived close to one another, the order seems to have had little trouble maintaining this basic rule. The two sexes ate in the same dining hall, but at different tables; they sat in separate parts of their meeting halls during services, and were not allowed to shake hands or touch, even during Shaker dances, which formed an important part of their worship.

Father Joseph was wise enough to realize, however, that a total and absolute separation of the sexes simply could

B. B. DUNLAVY.                                                                    E. M. SCOTT.

# OFFICE OF DUNLAVY & SCOTT,

——— MANUFACTURERS OF ———

## SHAKER PRESERVES, BROOMS & AROMATIC ELIXIR OF MALT,

### AND BREEDERS OF BLOODED STOCK, &c.

Mr. James D. Speake.   Pleasant Hill, Ky., May 2d         1884

Dear Sir being the Care Taker of the boys in
the Center Family at this place and having in my Charge
Clyde, and Charlie Ambrose whose Guardian, You are, I take
this liberty of addressing You a few lines. They are both
Very good boys and I trust they will not lose anything
in Character by living with us. I use all my efforts to
instil into the minds of the boys in my Charge, the
Necessity of being good while young, that when they grow
older they will not depart from it. Little Charlie is a
nice boy and I am Very much attached to him. He seems
So loving in his nature and he Calls Me Papa! I have
three little ones who all Sleep in my room, and all Call
Me Papa! Well I treat them as if they were mine. Charlie got
a letter a Short time ago from Your little Son Harold and
he was Very much pleased over it & I Suppose Katie will
answer it. Tell Harold that Charlie now wears pants and he
plays all day and Sleeps well at night. He is now in bed and
asleep while I am writing. Katie & Maude are all right and
well Contented. I take the liberty of Sending the love of all

(over)

not be maintained in a communal society. So he devised what was called the union meeting. Twice a week groups of from four to ten of each sex would meet. The participants were chosen by the elders and elderesses as being compatible. Seated about five feet from one another, they could converse freely on any suitable topic. Most observers found such meetings dull and the conversations shallow, but the Shakers themselves enjoyed their union meetings hugely, often joking, laughing, and singing.

There are a number of reasons why the apparently intolerable rule of celibacy was maintained with relative ease by the Shakers. First, the Shakers were organized into small face-to-face groups, and no individual was ever alone. Even the elders and elderesses worked in pairs to keep an eye on one another. The Shakers' day was thoroughly planned, down to the last minute, and there was no idle time. Perhaps more important was the quality of people who joined the order in the first place. Most, like Mother Ann, doubtless found sex disagreeable, and the avoidance of sex, far from being a burden, was a relief. Any who found celibacy too great a problem could easily withdraw from the order. The Shakers accepted only adults as full members, and before joining, most of the members must have had a fairly definite idea of the sort of lives they wished to lead. In the world, marriage was the norm, and there was really no suitable place for bachelors and single women. Those who could not or would not marry might easily be better off among the Shakers.

A visitor to a village of these enthusiastic celibates would have been surprised to find many children. Parents that

OPPOSITE: *Letter written in 1884 by the caretaker of the children at Pleasant Hill, Kentucky. The Shakers provided a home and school for orphans and foundlings in the hope that, upon becoming of age, they would become members of the Shaker faith.*

joined the order brought their children with them, though the children were raised by the community rather than by the parents. For years the Shakers also took in large numbers of orphans. It was with the young that the problem of celibacy became acute. Most of those who were raised in the society left it when they came of age. They were given a small sum of money and the blessings of the Shakers. Once in the outside world, however, some found themselves lost and unhappy and returned to the Shaker life, but many, probably the vast majority, departed for good.

To be successful, the orderly Shaker life had to provide at least one outlet for human emotions. This was their worship, but even here the uncontrolled emotionalism of the early days was ritualized. Dancing, some of it quite intricate and energetic, became a regular part of the Shaker meetings. The mass Shaker dances were famous, and throngs of visitors came to the public services to witness what they doubtless regarded as strange rites. For their part, the Shakers seem to have enjoyed the attention, and their public performances became highly skillful and theatrical. In the private family meetings, however, there was more leeway for emotionalism and individual expression.

The great spurts of growth of the Shakers are linked to religious revivals in other denominations. Many of those whose religious feelings and expectations had been aroused by the revivals were ripe for conversion to the Shaker way of life. The largest group of converts for the society came in the backwash of an extraordinary event known as the Kentucky Revival.

Starting around 1799 Kentucky and its neighboring regions were swept by the most frantic religious enthusiasm ever witnessed in America. These were frontier regions with few established churches for the settlers, who themselves were widely scattered. The religious needs of the settlers were served by traveling preachers, often uneducated and self-ordained, who spoke at great outdoor gatherings called camp meetings. Since travel to one of these meetings was usually arduous, they were expected to last several days and to give the worshippers enough "religion" to carry them through periods when no preachers were available. The camp meeting preacher who could not set his audience to crying, screaming, and fainting was considered a failure. In the hard and often dull life of the frontiersman, camp meetings were a major source of entertainment and emotional release.

Usually religious revivals burned themselves out after a few months. But the Kentucky Revival continued building for several years. Accounts of the Kentucky meetings were carried in the newspapers and were read with great interest by the New England Shakers, who sensed a magnificent opportunity to spread their doctrine.

A few Shaker missionaries traveled a thousand miles on foot to reach the center of the religious excitement. But opposition to the Shakers in Kentucky was fierce, more violent even than it had been in the early New England days. Shakers were regularly stoned, beaten, and arrested, and their homes, farm buildings and meetinghouses were often burned. Celibacy was a greater stumbling block among the rugged settlers than it had been in Puritan New England. Opponents of the Shakers eagerly spread stories about how the order castrated male members and indulged in wild orgies. The charges, although mutually exclusive, were often made in a single attack. But the Shaker message, that the millennium had come for those who joined the sect, had great appeal to the more radical among the disillusioned revivalists. The orderly Shaker way of life also was an attraction to those unable to tolerate the rough and uncertain pioneer existence.

As in New England, the farms of more prosperous converts often became the nuclei for new Shaker societies. By 1830 the Shakers had reached their peak—there were eighteen separate Shaker societies with a total membership of nearly six thousand people. They maintained this level and increased in prosperity until the time of the Civil War, thirty years later.

Although Shakers profited from revivals, they were not immune to the need for the revival spirit within their own ranks. Starting late in 1837 numbers of Shakers at Niskeyuna were suddenly seized by fits of shaking and whirling. Later many began to go into trances during which they sang, talked to angels, and described the visits that they made to heaven. These gifts, as the strange manifestations were called, spread from order to order, and within a year the excitement had gripped some members of every one of the eighteen Shaker societies.

By 1838 Shaker mediums, or spiritual communicators, were delivering messages from Mother Ann and Jesus. Messages also came in the name of Father Joseph, Mother Lucy, and many other departed Shakers. In addition, historical characters ranging from the Prophet Elijah and Alexander the Great to Washington and Napoleon seemed to seek contact with the Shakers. Ultimately messages were received from Almighty God and a strange and awesome figure called Holy Mother Wisdom.

The Shakers had always been attracted by people they considered exotic, primitive, or somehow different, perhaps because that is how the world regarded them. Indian spirits were prominent among those who visited Shaker mediums. Later came the spirits of Africans, Eskimos, and Chinese. When these spirits were around, the Shaker meetinghouses resounded with native songs and dances supposedly received directly from the spirit world. When possessed of an Indian spirit, the Shaker visionists rushed about waving imaginary tomahawks. Eskimo spirits set them to driving unseen sledges. When they were Turks, they acted barbarously, and

OPPOSITE: *A page from Shaker Almanac which advertised Shaker products for sale to "the world."*

SHAKERS PACKING AND SHIPPING SHAKER EXTRACT OF ROOTS, OR SEIGEL'S SYRUP, MT. LEBANON, N. Y.

## 9th MONTH.     SEPTEMBER, 1885.     30 DAYS.

| Day Yr | Day Mo | Day Wk | Chronological Events. | Portland, Nor N Y, Mich Wis, Minn, Iowa, Neb, Oregon, &c, Sun Rises | Sun Sets | Moon Rises | Conn, So N Y, Penn, Ohio, Ill, Mo, Kan, Utah, Nev, Cal, &c, Sun Rises | Sun Sets | Moon Rises |
|---|---|---|---|---|---|---|---|---|---|
| | | | | H. M. | H. M. | H. M. | H. M. | H. M. | H. M. |
| 244 | 1 | T | Battle of Sedan, 1870.......... | 5 26 | 6 34 | 10 43 | 5 27 | 6 32 | 10 47 |
| 245 | 2 | W | J. Howard born, 1726.......... | 5 27 | 6 32 | 11 34 | 5 28 | 6 30 | 11 39 |
| 246 | 3 | T | Thiers died, 1877.............. | 5 28 | 6 30 | morn. | 5 29 | 6 29 | morn. |
| 247 | 4 | F | French Republic procl'd, 1870 | 5 29 | 6 29 | 0 33 | 5 30 | 6 27 | 0 37 |
| 248 | 5 | S | Mobile taken, 1864............ | 5 30 | 6 27 | 1 37 | 5 31 | 6 25 | 1 41 |
| 249 | 6 | S | Lafayette born, 1757.......... | 5 31 | 6 25 | 2 46 | 5 32 | 6 24 | 2 50 |
| 250 | 7 | M | Buffon born, 1707............. | 5 32 | 6 23 | 3 58 | 5 33 | 6 22 | 4 0 |
| 251 | 8 | T | Sebastopol assaulted, 1855.... | 5 33 | 6 22 | sets. | 5 34 | 6 20 | sets. |
| 252 | 9 | W | Invasion of Canada, 1775...... | 5 34 | 6 20 | 6 50 | 5 35 | 6 19 | 6 51 |
| 253 | 10 | T | Naval Battle of Lake Erie, 1813 | 5 35 | 6 18 | 7 25 | 5 36 | 6 17 | 7 26 |
| 254 | 11 | F | Battle of Brandywine, 1777.... | 5 36 | 6 16 | 7 59 | 5 37 | 6 15 | 8 1 |
| 255 | 12 | S | Battle of Chepultepec, 1847... | 5 37 | 6 15 | 8 37 | 5 38 | 6 14 | 8 38 |
| 256 | 13 | S | Battl' of Quebec, 1759........ | 5 38 | 6 13 | 9 12 | 5 39 | 6 12 | 9 16 |
| 257 | 14 | M | Wellington died, 1852........ | 5 39 | 6 11 | 9 53 | 5 40 | 6 10 | 9 57 |
| 258 | 15 | T | Mexico captured, 1847......... | 5 41 | 6 9 | 10 36 | 5 41 | 6 9 | 10 41 |
| 259 | 16 | W | Moscow burned, 1812 | 5 42 | 6 8 | 11 23 | 5 42 | 6 7 | 11 28 |
| 260 | 17 | T | Battle of Antietam, 1862..... | 5 43 | 6 6 | morn. | 5 43 | 6 5 | morn. |
| 261 | 18 | F | Battle of Gravelotte, 1870.... | 5 44 | 6 4 | 0 13 | 5 44 | 6 4 | 0 18 |
| 262 | 19 | S | President Garfield died, 1881... | 5 45 | 6 2 | 1 6 | 5 45 | 6 2 | 1 10 |
| 263 | 20 | S | Robert Emmet hung, 1803..... | 5 46 | 6 0 | 2 2 | 5 46 | 6 0 | 2 5 |
| 264 | 21 | M | Battle of Fisher's Hill, 1864.... | 5 47 | 5 59 | 2 59 | 5 47 | 5 58 | 3 2 |
| 265 | 22 | T | Walter Scott died, 1832 ..... | 5 48 | 5 57 | 3 58 | 5 48 | 5 57 | 4 0 |
| 266 | 23 | W | Andre arrested, 1780.......... | 5 49 | 5 55 | 4 58 | 5 49 | 5 55 | 4 59 |
| 267 | 24 | T | Battle of Monterey, 1846. ... | 5 50 | 5 53 | rises. | 5 50 | 5 52 | rises. |
| 268 | 25 | F | Ethan Allen captured, 1777.... | 5 51 | 5 52 | 6 45 | 5 51 | 5 52 | 6 46 |
| 269 | 26 | S | T. Clarkson died, 1846........ | 5 52 | 5 50 | 7 20 | 5 52 | 5 50 | 7 22 |
| 270 | 27 | S | Steamer Arctic lost, 1854..... | 5 53 | 5 48 | 7 58 | 5 53 | 5 48 | 8 1 |
| 271 | 28 | M | Sir W. Jones born, 1746....... | 5 55 | 5 46 | 8 41 | 5 54 | 5 47 | 8 45 |
| 272 | 29 | T | Lord Nelson born, 1758........ | 5 56 | 5 45 | 9 30 | 5 55 | 5 45 | 9 35 |
| 273 | 30 | W | Whitfield died, 1770.......... | 5 57 | 5 43 | 10 26 | 5 56 | 5 43 | 10 30 |

**MOON'S PHASES.**

| | PORTLAND, WEST. | NEW YORK, WEST |
|---|---|---|
| Third Quarter...... 2d. | 0h. 31m. a. m. | 0h. 19m. a. m. |
| New Moon......... 8th. | 3h. 59m. p. m. | 3h. 47m. p. m. |
| First Quarter..... 16th. | 1h. 31m. p. m. | 1h. 19m. p. m. |
| Full Moon........ 24th. | 3h. 11m. a. m. | 2h. 59m. a. m. |

They say that nobody ever dies in Nantucket, they simply dry up. "We ain't no chickens," said an old inhabitant the other day. "The boy next to me is ninety-three, I am eighty-nine; the boy on the other side of me is eighty-five, and the youngest sitting beyond is the baby, being only seventy-nine." Then they all began to discuss what they would do during the next ten years, and unanimously agreed, that should illness ever overtake them they would rely on the Shaker Extract of Roots, or Seigel's Syrup.

as Frenchmen they behaved with extravagantly polite manners. There was an unworldliness, almost a childlike quality, about this side of Shaker life.

During this period huge numbers of new songs and dances, even entire books, were said to be dictated by the spirits. Among the many strange rituals ordered by the spirits was the "sweeping gift." This was meant to cleanse Shaker dwellings and shops of evil spirits, which lived in dirt and dust. A group of mediums, preceded by singers and elders, marched throughout the community chanting, exhorting, and wielding spiritual brooms. The rest of the members devoted themselves to the actual job of cleaning. After any session of the "sweeping gift," the already spotless Shaker communities were said to be "fifty percent more tidy than usual."

These excitements gripped the Shakers for about ten years, and during part of that time the society closed itself off entirely from the outside world. Public worship was abandoned, and visitors were no longer welcome at Shaker villages. The Shakers were hopeful, but puzzled; they were trying to figure out what was happening, and what it meant.

The vast majority of Shakers were doubtless deeply moved by this period that was called Mother Ann's Work. But some of the more sophisticated leaders may well have been skeptical, if not downright cynical, about the various messages and gifts from beyond. Yet the period served a distinct purpose for the society. Peace and prosperity had introduced new temptations into Shaker life, and the underlying message of all the communications seems to have been the need to purge the order of all impurities, and to return to the original principles that had inspired Mother Ann and her followers.

Oddly, about ten years after spirit communications began among the Shakers, there was an outbreak of alleged spirit communication at the little town of Hydsville, New York. The fame of the Hydsville "rappings" spread very quickly, and it was the beginning of the movement known as modern spiritualism. Many Shakers became convinced spiritualists, and they noted with pride that the movement had really begun with them. But in later years some Shakers looked back upon the time of Mother Ann's Work with considerable embarrassment, and rejected the whole idea of spirit inspiration. A visitor discovered some books allegedly written under "spiritual guidance" in a Shaker reading room. "One of their [Shaker] elders declared that I ought never to have seen them, and that their best use was to burn them."

Whatever turmoil there was in the religious life of the Shakers, their villages, at the height of Shaker prosperity, presented to the world a picture of perfect peace and orderliness. An English traveler who visited Shaker communities in the mid-nineteenth century left this description:

"The streets are quiet; for here you have no grog shop, no beer house, no lock up, no pound; . . . and every building, whatever may be its use has something of the air of a chapel. The paint is all fresh; the planks are clean and bright; the windows are all clean. A sheen is on everything; a happy quiet reigns."

No one could fail to be impressed by Shaker ingeniousness. They were the inventors of the flat broom, which turned out to be one of their most popular sale items. They also claim to have invented the circular saw, and they created or improved hundreds of other laborsaving devices for home, shop, and farm.

Shaker inventions are part of the past, but Shaker furniture and architecture are inspiring even today. Everything they constructed was simple, but extremely well made. The frills and ornamentation so popular during the nineteenth century had no place in Shaker life. Following the doctrines first laid down by Father Joseph, they made everything in accordance with its order and use.

Some find in Shaker craftsmanship the most persuasive testimony to the success of the Shaker way of life. Observes

*Vaulted hallway leading to meeting room in the Centre Family House at Pleasant Hill, Kentucky.*

Professor Mark Holloway, "The facts of Shaker craftsmanship alone, deny unhappiness. No one who was frustrated, repressed, discontented, or ill-adjusted to life could have produced such simple and eloquent work, which breathes an air of tranquillity and fulfillment. It is only when we begin to cast an eye on the tortured furniture, the gaudy and tawdry trappings, and the grotesque upholstery of the 'world' at the same period that we can see the products of frustration and neurosis. Whatever psychologists might make of the peculiar religious attitude of the Shakers, the Shakers themselves found fulfillment in it."

Orderliness and ingeniousness continued to be features of Shaker life, even after the order went into decline. Indeed, they dominated the Shaker world, while religious passion faded. The period of Mother Ann's Work was the last flare-up of Shaker enthusiasm. But the edifice of the Shaker society that had been so painstakingly constructed appeared to be as strong as ever. In 1874 an American journalist named Charles Nordhoff was collecting information on American communistic societies. He visited as many of them as he was able, and of course he paid a visit to the Shakers, spending much time at the New Lebanon society. Though Shaker membership had ceased to increase, and even had declined a bit, Nordhoff saw no reason to believe that the society might not undergo another major period of growth; indeed many were predicting exactly that. But Nordhoff, almost unconsciously, seemed to sense that stagnation and fussiness had set in among the Shakers. He wrote:

"The floor of the assembly room was astonishingly bright and clean, so that I imagined it had been recently laid. It had, in fact, been used twenty-nine years; and in that time had been but twice scrubbed with water. But it was swept and polished daily; and the brethren wear to the meetings shoes made particularly for those occasions, which are without nails or pegs in the soles, and of soft leather. They have invented many such tricks of housekeeping, and I could

*Sieve hanging from a pinboard and typical Shaker seed boxes.*

see that they acted just as a parcel of old bachelors and old maids would, anywhere else, in these particulars—setting much store by personal comfort, neatness, and order; and no doubt thinking much of such minor morals."

While at New Lebanon, Nordhoff met Elder Frederick Evans, the best-known Shaker leader of his day. Elder Frederick was a worldly man for a Shaker. He traveled much and often wrote for the popular press. It was his aim to have his beloved society reach out more to the world, to become more relevant, as we might say today. Evans was born in England and migrated to America in 1820. In his youth he had been a materialist, a free thinker, and a radical socialist, and had written and edited a number of political journals. Frederick Evans was also an idealist, and in his search for social justice and the ideal community, he encountered the Shakers and was converted by them. But he continued to agitate for a variety of reforms, both within the Shaker society and in the world.

At one time the Shakers' only knowledge of the outside world came from carefully selected newspaper articles read to them once a week by one of the elders. Under Evans, newspapers, magazines, and books on travel, history, and science could be found in Shaker reading rooms. Musical instruments, flowers, and pictures, all once considered superfluities of the world, were introduced by Elder Frederick. He argued that the saints were as deserving of the good things of the world as were the sinners.

Elder Frederick was by no means the undisputed leader of the society, and his liberalizing innovations were opposed by many who believed that the Shakers could be held together best by a more rigid adherence to the austere practices of the past and a more complete separation from the world. But Elder Frederick, as the most prominent and active spokesman of the society, represented the thinking of the majority.

Elder Frederick admitted to Nordhoff that the Shakers had not been increasing in numbers, and in fact many societies had decreased. "But," wrote Nordhoff, "they [the Shakers] expected large accessions in the course of the next few years, having prophecies among themselves to that effect. Religious revivals he [Evans] regarded as 'the hotbeds of Shakerism'; they always gain members after a 'revival' in any part of the country."

Evans also admitted to Nordhoff that the attempt to raise children to the Shaker way of life had been a failure, and that few children were taken in anymore. "When men or women come to us at the age of twenty-one or twenty-two, then they make the best Shakers. The society then gets the man's or woman's best energies, and experience shows us that they have then had enough of the world to satisfy their curiosity and make them restful. Of course we like to keep up our numbers; but of course we do not sacrifice our principles."

Nor did they, though the society continued its slow decline, which at the present time is nearing its inevitable end. Numerous reasons have been advanced for the decline of the Shakers: poor financial management, a general reduction in the quality of leadership after the death of Mother Lucy, and less effective missionary efforts. But the most significant reason seems to have been that after the Civil War the country had changed, and the Shakers had not. The small, largely self-sufficient Shaker communes could not compete economically with the growing industries. The Shakers themselves began purchasing many of the world's goods that they had formerly made themselves, because buying was cheaper. The poor and dispossessed, who had once made up the core of Shaker converts, could now find a measure of economic security, if not happiness, in the new factories or in the new lands opening up farther to the west.

The whole Shaker way of life was against the temper of the times. An English journalist who studied the Shakers questioned some of those outside the society as to what they thought of it. One reply he received seems to get to the heart of the matter:

"We Americans love liberty too well to join such societies as these. What are they but pure despotisms, where all are subject to the will of one man, a few leaders, or even a woman? Are not these places opposed to science and all improvements? We Americans are a go-ahead people, not to be confined anywhere or stopped by anything."

The "go-ahead" Americans were less interested in religion than they previously had been. True enough, church mem-

*Sister Elizabeth, a member of the present-day Shaker community at Sabbathday, Maine.*

bership remained high, and there were periodic revivals—but the deep commitment and agonized soul-searching were largely missing. The revivals that had once swelled the Shaker ranks became mechanical exercises in ritual piety. Run by business-oriented figures like Dwight Moody, and backed by businessmen, these new revivals were aimed at making Christians content with the world.

The Shakers were isolated from all of the trends of post-

Civil War America. They had no connection with lay organizations, no mother church except the society itself, and no systematic method of recruitment. In contrast to the Shakers, the number of Americans in Catholic monastic orders rose after 1860. The Shakers simply waited for whatever recruits appeared at their communities, and the recruits never came in sufficient numbers to keep the society vibrant enough to take advantage of any change that might take place in the national mood.

The Shakers have become part of history. Visiting one of their surviving communities today is a bittersweet experience. They are still lovely places, particularly when compared to the hideous suburban sprawl that has grown up elsewhere. They are reminders that America could indeed be beautiful. Restored Shaker communities at Hancock, Massachusetts, and Pleasant Hill, Kentucky, are run for the benefit of tourists. There are Shaker museums in the Shaker Heights area of Cleveland and at Old Chatham, New York. Genuine Shaker furniture commands astronomical prices in antique shops, and extensive exhibits of Shaker crafts may be seen at the Smithsonian Institution in Washington, D.C., the Boston Museum of Fine Arts, and many other museums. The early followers of Ann Lee could hardly have imagined that the Shaker name would become so respectable to the world. Perhaps it is fortunate that they did not know.

Whatever the Shakers' shortcomings—and they were legion—this unworldly yet practical, gentle yet passionate, sect filled a deep need for the thousands who joined it. The need for serenity, order, sharing, and spiritual fulfillment still exists today, but the Shakers' day is done. Whether, as Sister Bertha predicted, "someone will pick up the way," only time will tell.

# 4 🌿 The German Communes

Much of the history of the communal movement in America was made by German immigrants. One of the earliest communal societies in the New World, The Woman in the Wilderness, was made up of Germans. One of the longest lived, the Ephrata Cloister, was also a community of Germans. Right now the largest communal society in America, indeed the largest communal group in the entire Western world, is the German-speaking Hutterites of the western United States and Canada. Between the time of The Woman in the Wilderness and the Hutterites, there were a number of other notable German communal societies. Only the Shakers, an English and American development, ever matched the German communes in size and longevity.

The German communal movement grew out of religion. In Germany the nonconformist Protestant movements, such as Anabaptism and Pietism, were the wellsprings for communal life. These movements tended to ignore theology and to concentrate on "living a Christian life." Often this meant separating oneself from the world and adopting a communal life as described in the Book of Acts. Scores of sects sprung up, usually around an "inspired" leader. Since most of these sects did not allow their young men to serve in the army, refused to pay taxes, and were generally disrespectful of any authority other than the word of God as they interpreted it, they were often persecuted, both by the state and the established church. Some fought back, as did the Anabaptists at Munster. But most looked to the sayings of Jesus for their response—"And whosoever shall not receive you, nor hear your words, when ye depart out of that house or city, shake off the dust of your feet." The persecuted sects shook off the dust of their feet and moved on.

Many came to the New World during the eighteenth and nineteenth centuries. The most well known of these German immigrants are the Old Order Amish, often called the Pennsylvania Dutch (a misnomer since they are German, not Dutch, and since there are now more Amish in Wisconsin than in Pennsylvania). Although the Amish live cooperative, rather than communal, lives they are in many ways typical of the German communalists. They are the "plain people" who live simply and revere hard work. By dress, language, and custom they try to remain rigidly separated from the outside world, which they see as full of Godless temptations.


## THE RAPPITES

George Rapp was one of the most successful leaders of the German communities that migrated to America. He was born in 1757, the son of a small farmer in Württemberg, Germany. He received a moderate amount of schooling, assisted his father on the farm, and worked as a weaver during the winter months. At the age of twenty-six he married, and his wife bore him a son and a daughter. All in all, he seemed a very ordinary man. But George Rapp was an individual in whom the religious fires burned fiercely. He was a devoted student of the Bible, and the more he read the more he became disgusted with the religious and social conditions of his neighbors. Clearly they were not living according to the precepts laid down by Jesus and the Apostles.

By the time he was thirty years old, Rapp had gathered a following of like-minded neighbors, and he began to preach sermons in his own home on Sundays. There were others who preached as Rapp did, and the established Lutheran clergy regarded them all as dangerous heretics. Rapp and his followers were fined, imprisoned, and generally harassed. Rather than discouraging the sect, persecution actually seemed to strengthen the Rappites, and they grew into a substantial body of three hundred families.

In addition to his preaching, Father Rapp, as he came to be called, seems to have been an able farmer and a good businessman. By 1803 he had accumulated enough money through his own efforts, and those of his followers, to sail to America to find land where he and his fellow believers could live as they pleased, free from persecution. Rapp purchased five thousand acres in Pennsylvania north of Pittsburgh. In 1804 six hundred Rappites arrived from Germany. In Germany they had been small farmers and artisans, and their skills were much appreciated in America. During the first winter Rapp took fifty of his best workmen to the land he had purchased, to build dwellings for the colony. The remainder found work on farms and in the towns throughout Maryland and Pennsylvania. In 1805 the Rappites gathered together on their newly purchased land and formed the Harmony Society. They named their village Harmony. According to the formal charter, the principles of the society, "being faithfully derived from the Sacred Scriptures, include the government of the patriarchal age, united to the community of property adopted in the days of the Apostles." It was to be a society with an autocratic leadership and a communal economy. Properly the community should be called the Harmony Society, but they were so closely bound to their founder that they were usually called Rappites.

It appears that the Rappites did not originally plan for a communal society. When they moved onto their new land, they found many among them who were sick and unable to support themselves, or who were too poor to make any financial contribution to the society. The communal way of life was adopted out of convenience. The Rappite community was primarily agricultural, but they also had a number of small industries—a saw mill, a tannery, and rather unusual for a communal society, a distillery. It was named the Golden Rule Distillery and was famed for the quality of its whisky. The Rappites themselves drank very little whisky, and sold most of their output. This was an activity that gave them a bad reputation among more abstemious Christians. In addition, the Rappites enjoyed wine and beer and were prodigious eaters, consuming four or five large meals a day.

There certainly seemed nothing very ascetic about Father Rapp's followers, and yet deep religious emotions must have lain beneath the placid surface of Rappite life. In 1807 the community was gripped by a religious fervor, and they resolved to adopt the rule of celibacy, which they believed conformed more closely with the teachings of Jesus. According to some accounts, the move to adopt celibacy was begun by some of the younger members of the community, and though Father Rapp was not adverse to such a development, he advised caution. Less friendly observers insist that Father Rapp forced his followers to give up sex, after he had reached an age at which he was no longer interested in it.

The Rappites abandoned marriage with remarkable ease. They made no special rules about the separation of men and women. Couples who had been married continued to live together in the same house if they wished, "only treating each other as brother and sister in Christ." A certain number of Rappites, particularly younger ones, could not abide the new rule of celibacy and quit the community. Still, no group has ever changed from the married to the celibate state with

*George Rapp, from a painting made when he was approximately eighty years old.*

such apparent tranquillity. At the same time that they adopted celibacy, the Rappites also gave up the use of tobacco. "A deprivation," commented the historian of communities Charles Nordhoff, "which these Germans must have felt almost as severely as the abandonment of conjugal joys."

The Rappites had no interest in making converts, so by their own rules they were doomed to extinction in one generation. This did not worry them a bit since Father Rapp had repeatedly proclaimed that Judgement Day would come within his own lifetime, and that he would personally lead his followers before God.

By hard work and frugal living the Rappite community at Harmony became fairly prosperous. But the site, from the Rappite point of view, was far from perfect. The soil, for example, was unsuitable for growing grapes. So in 1814 the Rappites purchased a new site in the Wabash River valley of Indiana, and sold their original settlement. In Indiana Rappite prosperity continued to increase, and so, despite the rule of celibacy, did the size of the community. About one hundred of Rapp's followers who had stayed in Germany came over. By 1817 the Rappite community had reached its high point of nearly nine hundred members. By 1818 the Rappites had become so prosperous and so satisfied with their way of life that, by unanimous consent, they burned the book in which was recorded the amounts each family had originally contributed to the community.

Harmony, Indiana, grew into an important commercial center, but still Father Rapp and his followers were displeased with the location of their earthly paradise. The climate seemed unhealthy to them, and they had poor relations with the rough farmers and trappers who were their neighbors. So in 1824 they sold the village to the wealthy English social reformer Robert Owen, and they purchased another tract of land near Pittsburgh, in the vicinity of their original home. With the experience gained from building two previous communities, Rapp's followers made their new home, named Economy, a model village. One wonders if the change in names, from the more spiritual Harmony to the rather commercial Economy, reflected some change in values within the community.

To the outsider, the most attractive feature of Rappite life was their easygoing, nonfanatical attitude. Like the Shakers in their later days, the Rappites did everything possible to insure personal comfort. Their homes were neat, well-heated, and even enjoyed the luxury of carpets. They dressed plainly but comfortably. In the area of food the Rappites clearly enjoyed themselves, and as a result most were quite stout. The various holy days were celebrated with great feasts that would have done credit to a more self-indulgent folk. Father Rapp also encouraged his followers to love music and flowers. Reading, however, was generally limited to the Bible and selected religious works.

Agriculture was a very highly prized labor in the community. Rapp himself often worked in the fields. But the place of the mechanic and artisan was not forgotten. Everything possible was done to make work lighter and more pleasant. The Rappites, like the Shakers, were very ingenious at inventing laborsaving devices. Also like the Shakers, the Rappites loved to work, but hated to work too hard. Hired hands usually turned out more work in a day than did the Rappites themselves. Even their religious services were not overly long or taxing.

Most of those who visited the Rappites at Economy concluded that they had succeeded in establishing a limited, but very real utopia for themselves. The Duke of Saxe-Weimar, who observed various communes during a tour of America in 1826, wrote lyrically about the Rappites:

"Their factories and workshops are warmed during the winter by means of pipes connected with the steam-engine. All the workmen and especially the females had healthy complexions, and moved me deeply by the warm-hearted

*Barbara Bosh, last female member of the Rappites' Harmony Society. She died in 1905.*

friendliness with which they saluted the elder Rapp. I was also much gratified to see vessels containing sweet-scented flowers standing on the machines. The neatness which universally reigns is in every respect worthy of praise."

But praise of Father Rapp was not universal. Critics contended that he was a ruthless old autocrat who deliberately kept his people in superstitious ignorance, so that he could exercise complete control over them. They complained that he employed such devices as a secret tunnel, so that it would appear he could be in two places at one time. It was even said that Rapp had arranged the murder of his own son John because John had displeased him. Whatever the truth of such charges, it does seem that there was a strong current of dissatisfaction with Rapp, for in 1831 there was a serious split within the community.

The cause of the split was a German religious racketeer named Bernhard Muller, who styled himself Count Maximilian de Leon. In 1831 the bogus count and a little band of followers arrived at Economy and were allowed to stay at the community. Within a few weeks de Leon had gathered his own party inside the village. De Leon commanded the loyalty of about two hundred and fifty people at Economy, while about five hundred remained behind Father Rapp. From the Book of Revelation, the old patriarch found an appropriate quote to cover the situation. "And [the dragon's] tail drew the third part of the stars of heaven, and did cast them to the earth. . . ."

The "third part" was cast out of Economy in the summer of 1832, but a financial settlement was worked out, and de Leon's followers relinquished all further claims on the Harmony Society. De Leon made an unsuccessful attempt to set up a colony of his own, led his followers to Louisiana, and died of cholera in 1834.

So sound was the prosperity of the Rappites that the loss of a third of their membership and a considerable sum of money affected them hardly at all.

Father Rapp, who was sure that he would not die, lived on and on in vigorous good health for so long that it appeared he might be right. Finally when he was dying at nearly ninety in 1847, he said, "If I did not know that the dear Lord meant I should present you all to Him, I should think that my last moment's come." These were his last words.

The community had been totally dependent upon Father Rapp, but the foundation he laid for communal life was sturdy enough to survive his death for nearly fifty years. When Nordhoff visited Economy in 1874, it was a village of old people, vigorous, healthy, and altogether admirable old people, but old people nonetheless. "The Harmonists themselves," he wrote, "are sturdy, healthy-looking men and women, most of them gray haired; with an air of vigorous independence; conspicuously kind and polite; well fed and well preserved."

Unlike the celibate Shakers who continued to hope for converts, the Rappites sought no new members. Nordhoff found that this society of old people talked little of the future. "The people look for the coming of the Lord; they await the appearance of Christ in the heavens; and their chief aim is to be ready for this great event, when they expect to be summoned to Palestine, to be joined to the great crowd of the elect."

The society was dissolved in 1905, and the last Rappite died in 1921.

## THE SEPARATISTS

At about the time that Father Rapp was planning to lead his followers out of Württemberg, Germany, to America, another group of Württemberg dissenters was experiencing severe persecutions. These were the Separatists, whose doctrines regarding a simple Christian life were similar to those of Father Rapp. But the Separatists were more aggressive in their denunciations of worldly sinfulness, and hence more open to official censure and punishment. After some years of enduring imprisonment, fines, and continual harassment, the Separatists determined to move to America, but they lacked the funds. Their plight came to the attention of a group of English Quakers, who not only helped to finance their emigration in 1817, but also aided them in purchasing a tract of land in Ohio where they could settle. They named their colony Zoar.

Originally the Separatists, like the Rappites, had no clear plan for forming a communal society. But the two hundred and fifty poor German immigrants found that if they did not pool their resources, they would be unable to survive as a distinct group.

The leading figure among the Separatists, Joseph Bäumeler, or Bimeler, as the name came to be spelled in America, was by all accounts an able man, but not a very lively one. He loved to deliver long lectures on religion, economy, morality, health, and other subjects. The Separatists were careful to call these sessions lectures rather than sermons, a term that smacked too much of the established church. After Bimeler's death his lectures were collected into three huge volumes, which were read regularly for the edification of the community members.

Though their neighbors often called these German communalists "Bimelers," Bimeler himself never held the commanding position in the community that Rapp held in his. Perhaps because they lacked a really strong leader, the Separatists remained one of the most democratic of the early German communities.

The first years in America were very difficult for the community, but in 1827 they had a stroke of good fortune. A canal was dug near Zoar, and they contracted to do part of the work for $21,000. This money, along with the money made by selling their produce to the contractors, enabled the Separatists to pay off all their debts, and they were never again threatened by poverty.

Originally the Separatists had planned a celibate community, but around 1830 they decided to permit marriage to ensure their continual survival. Although marriage was permitted, Bimeler made it clear that it was a distinctly inferior spiritual state. In the *Principles of the Separatists* written by Bimeler, one of the tenets was, "All intercourse of the sexes, except what is necessary to the perpetuation of the species we hold to be sinful and contrary to the order and command of God. Complete virginity or entire cessation of sexual commerce is more commendable than marriage."

Bimeler himself married and raised a family, and it was rumored that he had encouraged the community to abandon celibacy because of his attraction to a young woman who had been assigned to wait upon him. However, one must remember that scandalous tales of this type have been whispered about virtually every communal leader.

True to their name, the Separatists wished to remain as separate from the New World as they had from the Old. They married only within their community. Anyone who married an outsider was forced to leave the society. Children lived with their parents until they were three years old, when they were placed in special houses, one for boys and one for girls. From then on, they were under the control of the community, rather than their biological parents. The Separatists were especially adamant about not having their children educated in the schools of Babylon, as they referred to the outside world.

Life at Zoar followed a distinct routine. The community members rose at six in the winter or dawn in the summer. Breakfast was served shortly thereafter, the midday meal was eaten at noon, and supper was at six in the evening. The members also ate regular between-meal "bites," particularly in the summer when laboring in the fields. They drank cider and beer, but were forbidden stronger liquor, and were not supposed to smoke, though some of the men did so secretly. The people of Zoar worked hard all day and went to bed at nine. They lived in separate houses, each containing several families. Every family did its own cooking, but they obtained bread from a central bakery. The Separatists' main relaxation was reading the Bible and Bimeler's somber discourses. Religious music was permitted, but it was rather unimaginative, and no form of dancing or other light entertainment was allowed.

In economic terms the Separatists of Zoar were a success; they survived, kept their way of life pure from the contamination of the world, and even became prosperous. But they seem an incredibly dull and unattractive group, when compared with the Rappites, who had come from a similar background and held many of the same beliefs.

When Nordhoff visited Zoar in 1874, he found a community of three hundred self-satisfied middle-aged people. Bimeler had died in 1853, but thirty or forty of the original immigrants were still alive. The society had few converts, and made no great effort to gain more. Some of the young stayed with the group, but the majority departed to take up life in the world, as soon as they were able.

Nordhoff was not impressed by what he saw. He found the people "dull and lethargic." He wrote:

"The Zoar communists belong to the peasant class of Southern Germany. They are therefore unintellectual; and they have not risen in culture beyond their original condition. Nor were their leaders men above the general level of the rank and file; for Bäumeler has left upon the society no marks to show that he strove for or desired a higher life here, or that he in the least valued beauty, or even what we Americans call comfort. The little town of Zoar, though founded fifty-six years ago, has yet no foot pavements; it remains without regularity of design; the houses for the most part in need of paint; and there is about the place a general air of neglect and lack of order, a shabbiness . . . which shocks one who has but lately visited the Shakers and the Rappists."

Despite this profoundly negative judgement, when Nordhoff compared the life of the Separatists with that lived by their neighbors, he concluded, "that rude and uninviting as the life in Zoar seemed to me, it was perhaps still a step higher, more decent, more free from disagreeables, and upon a higher moral scale, than the average life in the surrounding country."

The community at Zoar plodded onward, its inhabitants growing increasingly old and quarrelsome. Finally in 1898 it dissolved amid an acrimonious controversy over money and land.


AMANA

The richest and most practical of American communal societies had its roots deep in religious mysticism. The founders of the Amana community were the Inspirationists. Their leaders were said to be the inspired "instruments" of God. *Werkzeuge*, "those who show forth the works of the Lord," they were called by their followers. The Inspirationists could trace the stream of divine inspiration back to the sixteenth century. There was no way of telling who the inspired instrument might be in any given generation, and sometimes the stream of inspiration lapsed for a period of years, and there were no leaders.

The greatest of these instruments was undoubtedly a former carpenter named Christian Metz. He was a tiny man, barely five feet tall, but he spoke with a fierce intensity and had a voice so powerful that it could be heard half a mile away. In 1842, when Metz was forty-nine years old, he received a great inspiration.

"Thus saith the Lord!" he cried. "Your goals and your

way leads towards the west, to the land which is still open to you and your friends. Behold, I am with you to lead you over the sea! Lay hold on Me, call upon Me, when the storms of temptation arise. Go now, four of you, endowed with full power to act for all the members, and to purchase land where you deem best."

Accordingly, Metz and three associates sailed to New York and purchased five thousand acres near Buffalo, at an exceptionally favorable price. The Inspirationists counted among their membership several wealthy people, including one who contributed $50,000 for the founding of the colony in America. Few societies were able to command such resources from the start. Over the next three years some eight hundred German Inspirationists followed their leader to Eben-Ezer, as their colony was named.

When they left Germany, the Inspirationists had no particular intention of establishing a communal society. But once in America they found what other religious sects had discovered—that communal living was the most practical way of holding the group together. Metz received the timely inspiration that all his followers should pool their wealth and live together in a community. The communal organization gave the Inspirationists the capital to build small workshops. Many of the people had been artisans and mechanics in Germany and would have been unhappy with strictly agricultural work.

The community was a financial success almost from the beginning. Four villages were built on community land—Lower, Middle, Upper, and New Eben-Ezer. But the Inspirationists were not really happy with their colony. The world, in the form of the city of Buffalo, was far too close. Besides, land prices had become so high in the region that the cost of expansion was prohibitive. So they decided or, as they said, they were inspired to move farther west. The Inspirationists found what they considered an ideal location in Iowa, and they sold their entire New York estate for a profit,

*Early view of the Inspirationist community of Amana, Iowa.*

an unusually successful transaction for a communal society. In general, buildings constructed for communes are unsuitable for individual use and often must be sold at a considerable loss.

The move to Iowa was accomplished slowly, but with admirable efficiency. As a new village in Iowa was built, one in Eben-Ezer was abandoned. The first new village was laid out in 1855; the last in 1862. The name Amana was chosen for the new colony. It was taken from the Bible. In the Song of Solomon is the line, "Come with me from Lebanon, my spouse, with me from Lebanon! Look from the top of Amana!"

Although the people of Amana were not celibate, they did not really approve of marriage. Boys and girls were segregated while still very young, and the inspired advice of an early leader was often repeated to the boys: "Fly from the society of woman-kind as much as possible, as a very highly dangerous magnet and magical fire."

The women's dresses were made in the simplest style, and they wore black caps and shawls to make themselves look as unattractive as possible. Yet, marriages did take place, though they were solemn, even depressing, events, and the newly married couples were immediately degraded to the lowest of the three spiritual orders into which the community had been divided. Families that had three or more children were looked down upon. A two-child family was considered more holy, a one-child family more holy still. A childless marriage was praised as one where chastity reigned.

In some respects, however, the rules of the Amana society were the least severe of any of the early German communal colonies. Marriage outside of the community was allowed, though the couple was automatically excluded from membership and had to reapply. Converts were accepted, and many came, particularly other German immigrants. All prospective members were subjected to a thorough character investigation and a long period of initiation.

Life in Amana was simple, but not ascetic. Families lived in their own comfortable houses. They took their meals in a common dining room. Usually one dining room served forty or fifty individuals. Like the other German communalists, the people of Amana ate heartily, from four to six meals a day. In the dining halls men were separated from women, "to prevent silly conversation and trifling conduct." Children also had a table to themselves. Beer and wine were drunk in moderation, and the men enjoyed their pipes and chewing tobacco if they desired.

In general, the Inspirationists were quiet, sober, unimaginative, but extremely successful. Their industries continued to flourish, they lost relatively few of their younger members, and these losses were more than made up for by new converts. The people of Amana were well thought of by their neighbors, who regarded them as shrewd, but fair dealers. Nordhoff found them among the most contented groups that he had ever seen. In the 1870s they were reckoned far and away the largest and wealthiest of the communities in America, and they were still growing. And yet, Amana also ultimately failed. What had gone wrong?

There is no simple answer to the question, for the death of Amana came slowly. Perhaps the primary reason was that the "inspiration" that had built the community disappeared. Metz died in 1867. Since he had been regarded as the instrument of the Lord, his presence had given the people the faith that they were acting directly upon God's word. Though most spiritual and temporal affairs of Amana were handled by groups of trustees, appointed by the community as a whole, all painful controversies could be referred to the Werkzeuge, who would resolve them by inspiration. No one could argue with the word of God.

One of the community members described how, during the regular Saturday meetings, "Brother Metz used to walk about in the meeting with his eyes closed; but he always knew to whom he was speaking, or where to turn with words of reproof, admonition, or encouragement." The presence of such a leader was invaluable in binding the community together.

After Metz's death the mantle of inspiration fell upon Barbara Heinemann (or Heynemann). She was the most unusual Werkzeuge in the sect's history. Normally women had no power at all within the group, but Barbara Heinemann became absolute leader. She was an illiterate serving girl who had once been expelled from the society for "casting too friendly an eye upon the young men." She was readmitted after two years, but again fell into disgrace after she married

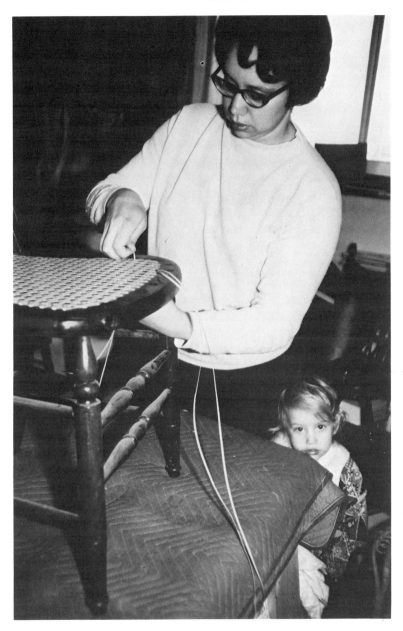

*A furniture worker in present-day Amana.*

George Landmann, though she continued to be known by the name of Heinemann. Ultimately she regained her standing and became the last great inspired instrument.

Barbara Heinemann died in 1883, and the stream of inspiration died with her. No other leader of comparable stature ever came forth. In the years that followed, the communal constitution of Amana was changed gradually, until in 1932 the community was converted to a joint stock company by a vote of the membership.

Amana is, of course, still there physically. The seven Iowa villages with their quaint old churches and shops are now a popular stopover for tourists. But they are no more a real commune than the restored cloister at Ephrata. The descendants of the original Amana communists are quite wealthy, and the name of the community is found on a line of electrical appliances manufactured by a company owned by the Amana descendants.

BETHEL AND AURORA

Not all of the German communal societies were imported directly from Germany. At least one formed among Germans already in the United States. This community was gathered together by an unlikely leader named Dr. Keil. He was a German-born mystic, hypnotist, and quack healer. For some time he had supported himself as a physician in New York and Pittsburgh. He claimed to be the owner of a mysterious volume, written in human blood, containing the recipes for medicines that enabled him to cure all sorts of diseases. When he became a Methodist, he burned the strange book after chanting the proper incantations and spells. Finally, Dr. Keil formed a sect of his own and announced that he was one of the two witnesses to the Second Coming of Christ mentioned in the Book of Revelation, and that he would be slain in the presence of his followers.

*The Bethel commune, Missouri.*

In 1833 the ranks of Keil's followers were swelled by some of those who had left the Rappites with the bogus, and recently deceased, Count de Leon. Perhaps it was the former Rappites who encouraged Keil to found a new community along Rappite lines, but without the rule of celibacy. In 1844 they secured twenty-five hundred acres in Missouri and set up the community of Bethel. At first the community members suffered from deprivation and a great deal of illness—a cruel blow in view of Dr. Keil's alleged qualifications. But by sheer dogged hard work and extreme frugality, they began to flourish in a modest way. In ten years the community doubled its acreage and population, reaching a height of about six hundred and fifty members. The communalists farmed and ran some small mills and a distillery.

Dr. Keil was the absolute leader of Bethel, and one might imagine that a man with his exotic background would create an unusual community. But, in fact, Bethel was run very much along the lines of Harmony or Zoar. Even the religion taught by Dr. Keil was familiar German nonconformist doctrine.

Around 1855 Keil seems to have become restless, and he began to envision a much larger community farther to the west. In 1856, with an advance party of eighty, he set out for the Pacific Coast, and established the community of Aurora in Oregon, about fifty miles south of Portland. About two-thirds of the original inhabitants of Bethel followed their leader to Oregon. Again they faced the usual hardships faced by any new community, and again by sheer persistence the German communitarians managed to carve out an adequate life for themselves.

But at Aurora, as at Bethel, the members never rose above a rather mediocre standard, nor did they ever seem to desire to rise any higher. Life was simple and unadorned. The villages, even in the best of times, looked shabby and haphazard. There were no sidewalks, and pigs foraged among the houses. The people of Aurora and Bethel never showed a hint of the craftsmanship and cleverness displayed by the Shakers, and they were far less industrious than the Rappites or the people of Amana. One notable feature was their preoccupation with medicine. Tiny Bethel contained two drugstores, one of which, according to an observer, was "large enough . . . to accommodate with purges and cathartics a town of twenty-five hundred inhabitants." At the time Bethel had about two hundred inhabitants.

Although Dr. Keil's followers reached a level of moderate comfort, it is likely that had they gone out to work on their own, most would have fared better economically. Nor did the community seem to offer any extraordinary spiritual or intellectual benefits to its members. Education of children was meager. There were regular Sunday religious services, but no great religious fervor. There were no regular hours of work and no regular form of government; indeed, there were few rules or structures of any kind in these communities. Dr. Keil was the leader, but he did not command the same respect as Rapp or Metz.

Yet somehow it all worked. The people seemed contented, there were very few disputes, and membership remained stable. However uninspiring and even unpleasant Aurora and Bethel looked to outsiders, the life there satisfied those who lived within their confines. But even these placid, slow-moving communities needed something to hold them together, and the force was Dr. Keil. When he died in 1877, there was no one in either community to take his place. Bethel dissolved in 1880, and Aurora, a year later.

## THE HUTTERITES

In today's world the Hutterites remain an amazing anachronism. Their roots go back to the same German religious tradition that had molded the Rappites, Separatists, Amanas, Amish, and other German nonconformists. But, from the beginning, the Hutterites seem to have been a communal group. The first Hutterite colony, or *Bruderhof*, was established in 1528 in Austerlitz, Moravia, a region in present-day Czechoslovakia. The name of the sect comes from an early leader, Jacob Hutter, who was burned at the stake in 1536. By the end of the sixteenth century there may have been as many as twenty thousand Hutterites.

These quiet, plain-living pacifistic farmers wanted nothing more from the world than to be left alone to pursue their own way of life. But the world kept intruding. At the end of the sixteenth century their lands became a battleground in the war between Austria and Turkey, and the Hutterites

*Inside a typical Hutterite house.*

were victimized by both sides. By 1622 they had been driven from Moravia into the neighboring states of Transylvania and Slovakia. But there the Roman Catholic Church began demanding that they convert, which many did. The remainder were forced to flee across the border to Wallachia, only to be caught in the middle of the Russo-Turkish War in 1788. Russia welcomed the Hutterites, though by that time the battered sect was down to a mere one hundred and twenty-three members. This remnant accepted the invitation to pioneer the plains of the Ukraine.

They prospered in Russia and increased in numbers for a century, but again the world intruded. The Russian government tried to induct members of the sect into the army, so once again they decided to move. In 1847 the eight hundred

LEFT: *Washday at the simple, well built Hutterite homes.*
RIGHT: *These girls wear long print dresses and scarves, but can go barefooted on warm days.*

Hutterites began a migration to South Dakota, into an area of open plains, not unlike the land they had farmed in the Ukraine. About half of the immigrants abandoned communal life in America when they were offered free land under the Homestead Act. The Homestead Act did not apply to communal groups, so the remaining Hutterites purchased enough land for three colonies.

The Hutterite migration went virtually unnoticed at first. The bearded, simply dressed men and their wives, clad in old-fashioned dresses and shawls, didn't look all that different from other pioneering folk. They spoke German and kept to themselves, but this too was not unusual in a nation of immigrants, particularly on the South Dakota frontier. In fact, for quite a while, their neighbors were not even aware that these German immigrants lived communally. When people thought of them at all, it was assumed that they were some sort of "Pennsylvania Dutch." Mostly they were just referred to as "those people."

For years the Hutterites were left alone, and they flourished. They were not celibate like the Rappites, and unlike the Inspirationists, they did not look upon the absence of children as a sign of godliness. Big families are useful to farmers, and the Hutterites have one of the highest birthrates of any group in the world.

When World War I began, the Hutterites were noticed, not only by their neighbors, who by that time generally disliked and distrusted them, but also by the federal government, which wanted to induct their young men into the army. A number of Hutterites were jailed as conscientious objectors, and two died while imprisoned at Fort Leavenworth. Neighbors, fired by what they said was patriotism, raided Hutterite cattle and sheep, because the Hutterites refused to fight or buy Liberty Bonds, and because they spoke German. Faced with the same persecution they had found in the Old World, the Hutterites decided to move across the border into Canada's western provinces. Between the end of World War I and the end of World War II, only a small number of Hutterites remained in the United States, but today a reverse migration is taking place. The attitude toward conscientious objectors is much more favorable in the United States now than it was a half century ago. Besides, in Canada, restrictive laws concerning the amount of land that can be purchased by the communal society have been passed. Individual farmers have a genuine fear of being overrun by these extremely successful and prolific communal farmers.

In the century since they first became established in North America, the Hutterites have lost only about five hundred members to the world, and many defectors have returned after finding themselves unhappy with life outside the community. Undoubtedly the fact that the Hutterite communities are located in the Great Plains of the United States and Canada, which are still relatively isolated areas, has helped the Hutterites hold their children, but still the record is an impressive one.

Like most of the German communalists of the past, the Hutterites live plain, but comfortable lives. Their dress is simple, the men wearing jackets and coats with checked shirts for work, and white shirts for church or prayer meeting. The women wear long patterned dresses, aprons, and head scarves. In dress, they resemble the more familiar Old Order Amish, to whom they are often compared. In fact, there are great differences between the two groups. The Amish are not communal and resolutely reject all modern inventions. They still drive about in horse-drawn buggies and refuse to use electricity. The Hutterites, on the other hand, have cars, telephones, electric lights, and usually possess the most modern farm equipment. Hutterite men are generally excellent mechanics, as well as farmers.

The Hutterites, however, are forbidden such forms of electronic entertainment as radio, television, and movies, and the age-old prohibition on dancing and the playing of musical instruments also is strictly enforced.

When a Hutterite colony grows to more than about one hundred and thirty members, they branch out. Generally the colonists try to buy a tract of land a few miles away. Since they have virtually free labor, the Hutterites have a buying power well beyond that of an individual farmer. Each colony is run by a boss, its temporal leader, and a preacher, its spiritual leader, and though every colony is theoretically independent, the entire Hutterite community will act in unison when necessary.

Hutterite religious practices are simple, yet all pervasive. Meetings are held several evenings a week and on Sunday. These consist of Bible reading, hymn singing, and sermons by the preacher, all in German, of course. The real strength of the Hutterite religion, however, comes from the tight-knit, conservative nature of Hutterite society. The preacher's authority is unquestioned, and there is little that goes on in the community that the preacher does not know about. Hutterite preachers are not adverse to condemning openly and loudly one of their flock for even a minor deviation from accepted practice. Like other German communitarians, the Hutterites have little interest in theology, though they often quote the Book of Acts to justify their communal way of life.

A serious problem for the Hutterites today is marriage between close relatives. The society's current population of over twenty thousand is descended from just a few families, and no marriage outside the Hutterite community is tolerated. To complicate matters further, the Hutterites are divided into three groups—Dariusleut, Lehrerleut, and Schmiedeleut. The first parts of the names refer to the founders of the three original colonies in South Dakota; *leut* means people. Differences between the three groups are barely noticeable to the outsider. One group wears more brightly colored clothes than the others, but that is about all. Yet marriage between members of different groups is rare in the rigid and traditional Hutterite society. Marriages between first cousins are not only common, but often necessary.

It is difficult to predict what the future holds for the Hutterites. They have withstood centuries of persecution, and are now more numerous, prosperous, and secure than ever before. Though prejudice against "the Hoots," as they are derisively called, continues, it is nothing compared to what they faced in the past.

But what of the more subtle dangers presented by the modern world? The Hutterites cannot entirely insulate their children from outside influences. The children go to school, though only to the minimum age required by the state. Schools in Hutterite communities usually are attended only by Hutterite children. Observers at the various colonies report that the boys often sneak off to see movies or buy tobacco—both forbidden by the strict Hutterite code. But still, the Hutterites have a way of life that has endured for a very long time, and so far they seem to be more than holding their own.

The danger to the Hutterite way of life is not so much that the communities will break up from dissatisfaction, but rather that they will fall victim to their own success and wealth, and ultimately be transformed into corporations like Amana. But here too the Hutterites have an advantage. The communal way of life was a convenience to many of the German sects. They did not even adopt it until after they had come to America. With the Hutterites, the community of goods is centuries old. They have also remained almost exclusively agricultural, rather than encouraging manufacturing, which would increase their contacts with the outside world. Whether Hutterite tradition is strong enough to stand in the face of worldly pressures, only time will tell.

# 5 🌿 Experiments and Excitements

## ROBERT OWEN AND NEW HARMONY

"I am come to this country to introduce an entire new system of society; to change it from an ignorant, selfish system to an enlightened social system which shall gradually unite all interests into one, and remove all causes for contest between individuals."

So announced the English social reformer Robert Owen, at the founding of his American community at New Harmony. The statement is so grandiose that it sounds funny now. But in April of 1825 few were inclined to laugh at Robert Owen. He had already accomplished much, and with his business ability, boundless enthusiasm, and large fortune it seemed that he might accomplish more, that he might indeed "introduce an entire new system of society."

Owen was the perfect self-made man. Born in 1771, the son of a poor saddler, he started work at the age of ten in the textile mills. By 1794 he had become a prosperous textile manufacturer. In 1800 Owen and his associates set up manufacturing operations at the town of New Lanark, in

Scotland. But Robert Owen was interested in much more than making money. Under his benevolent guidance New Lanark became a model industrial town. While most of the British working class of the nineteenth century was underpaid, undernourished, and illiterate, conditions were very different at New Lanark. The community had good housing, first-rate sanitation, nonprofit stores, and unusually pleasant working conditions, considering the times.

The success of Owen's reforms at New Lanark made him famous. He then set out to convert the world's governments and his fellow capitalists to his way of thinking. In 1819 the British government did pass some mild reforms that favored the workingman; these were a much adulterated version of proposals originally set forth by Robert Owen. But in general, Owen was severely disappointed with the reaction he received in Europe. Like so many others before him, Robert Owen turned his thoughts to establishing a model community in the New World.

Unlike most community founders, however, Owen had no need to build his community in the wilderness; he could buy one ready-made. In 1824 an agent acting for Father Rapp was visiting England trying to sell the Rappite village and land at Harmony, Indiana. There was nothing really wrong with Harmony. The Rappites had simply found it uncongenial and thought they would be happier if they moved back east again.

Owen had evolved an elaborate plan for what a proper community should look like. It was to consist of a connected series of buildings arranged in a hollow square, one thousand feet on each side. Schools, lecture rooms, libraries, and the like were to be given prominent places in this ideal community; the various domestic buildings, living quarters, and dining halls, though ample, were to be relegated to secondary positions. The scheme was far beyond even Robert Owen's means, and so he settled for the humble Rappite village and thirty thousand acres of land in Indiana. Owen was supremely confident that from this village his dream community would arise and spread "from Community to Community, from State to State, from Continent to Continent, finally overshadowing the whole earth, shedding light, fragrance and abundance, intelligence and happiness upon the sons of man."

Although most communitarians were religious people motivated by the vision of establishing God's kingdom on earth, Owen was a confirmed agnostic and followed a different vision. Man, he believed, was basically good; it was only bad environment that made him evil. Improve the environment and the man himself inevitably improves. His faith in the goodness of man, and the correctness of his own theories, was no less deep and unshakable than the faith of the Christian communitarians who thought they were living according to God's plan.

Owen's reputation as a reformer had preceded him to America. Upon his arrival he made a successful tour of the Eastern states, during which he lectured to huge audiences, and met with the most influential men in government and industry. He issued a public call to the "industrious and well-disposed of all nations" to come to his colony, now named New Harmony, so that the secular millennium he envisioned could begin.

Come the people did, but the problem was they were not all "industrious and well-disposed." Many of those attracted to New Harmony were genuine idealists fired by Owen's dreams. They had the will to begin a new community but lacked the skills. Others expected to find paradise ready and waiting for them, and were disappointed by the rude accommodations left by the Rappites. Within a few weeks eight hundred people from all classes, nationalities, and vocations had gathered at New Harmony. No one, no matter how undesirable or unsuitable he might have been, was barred from joining. Worst of all, this ill-assorted crowd had only the vaguest notion of what they were supposed

*Robert Owen, from a contemporary print.*

to do. The constitution framed by Owen for New Harmony was so vague as to be unworkable.

Owen himself was still busily lecturing and greeting admiring throngs in the East. When he did appear at New Harmony in April of 1825, he informed the community members that paradise would not commence immediately. New Harmony, he said, was a "halfway house" between a rational and irrational society. Owen himself would hold the title to the community for three years, after which all property was to be turned over to the community. In the meantime the communitarians would be paid nominal wages for their work. Owen thereupon departed for England and did not return to New Harmony for over six months.

The actual management of the community was left in the hands of a Preliminary Committee, and there is a good deal of dispute about exactly what took place during the period of Owen's absence. The community's newspaper, the *New Harmony Gazette,* was filled with optimistic stories and predictions, but in reality there was more confusion than progress. Some small industries were started, but agriculture was badly neglected. Owen's vision had little appeal to farmers, and few came to New Harmony. New recruits were still arriving at the community, and strenuous efforts were made to build new accommodations, but this was hampered by a shortage of skilled laborers. Still, New Harmony seemed to be on the move. It awaited only the return of Robert Owen to truly start on the road to a new society. Another Owenite community was also begun at Yellow Springs, Ohio.

When Owen did return to the United States at the end of 1825, he did not rush to New Harmony; rather he made another grand tour of the East to spread his doctrine. Nor did he have any new plans for the operation of New Harmony. What he did have was a huge and costly model of his ideal community, which had been constructed in England and lovingly transported across the ocean. This impressive but useless model was symbolic of Owen's attitude toward his community.

Owen finally arrived at the Indiana settlement near the end of January, 1826. He was followed by a group of distinguished educators and scholars, who arrived by riverboat and were dubbed "the Boatload of Knowledge." These men and women had been invited by Owen to join his enterprise.

New Harmony had progressed little since his departure, yet Robert Owen was carried away by enthusiasm. He announced that the halfway house concept, which was supposed to be a transformation period lasting three years, would be abandoned, and "a Community of Equality" would be established immediately. Unfortunately the people of New Harmony were so unprepared that they could not even agree upon electing an executive council to run the community, and within two weeks of the establishment of the Community of Equality, they appealed to Owen to resume personal control, which he did.

During Owen's absence New Harmony had closed its doors to new members and had made at least some attempt to get rid of the worst of the loafers and crackpots that had descended upon them. But the divisions in the community were deep. Owen was an agnostic, and many of his followers held similar opinions. But a large percentage of those at New Harmony were sincere Christians and were offended by Owen's increasingly outspoken criticism of religion. Owen was a nondrinker and tried to impose this principle upon the community. But some of his best workmen were also hard drinkers and not at all inclined to give up this pleasure. Worst of all were the class differences. The scholars who had arrived on the Boatload of Knowledge would not mix with the workingmen who formed the backbone of the community. Some of the intellectuals were shocked by the idea that they might have to engage in vulgar physical labor. Others tried, but failed. One of Owen's sons, Robert Dale Owen, noted in a diary, "I had previously tried one day's sowing wheat by hand, and held out until evening, but my right arm was comparatively useless for forty-eight hours thereafter." At the various balls and entertainments that were supposed to encourage friendship and brotherhood among the residents of New Harmony, an informal, but rigid segregation set in as the better educated middle class and the workers failed to mix.

Before New Harmony ever really got started, it began to break up. The first important defector was William Maclure, the distinguished American geologist and the brightest star in the Boatload of Knowledge. Maclure and his friends disliked Owen's agnosticism and made plans to form their own community. Owen granted them land about two miles from the village. This offshoot community, dubbed Macluria, lasted about nine months. A group of English farmers brought over by Owen were also granted land for their own community, where they could work and drink in peace. Finally New Harmony itself was officially divided into three separate communities. The changes satisfied no one, and disunity increased.

Despite snowballing problems Owen seemed convinced that a new age was dawning at New Harmony, and on July 4, 1826, he issued a Declaration of Mental Independence. It read in part:

"I now declare to you and to the world, that Man, up to this hour, has been in all parts of the earth a slave to a Trinity of the most monstrous evils that could be combined to inflict mental and physical evil upon his whole race. I refer to Private or Individual Property, Absurd and Irrational systems of Religion, and Marriage founded on Individual Property, and combined with some of these Irrational systems of Religion."

The *New Harmony Gazette* was thereafter dated in the first year of Mental Independence. This radical doctrine did nothing to ease the strains between Christians and non-Christians within the community. Many outsiders who had tolerated Robert Owen, the social reformer, began to agitate against Robert Owen, the free-love agnostic.

Constitution followed constitution at New Harmony in an attempt to find a workable plan for the community, but by the end of 1826 even Robert Owen's boundless optimism, and almost boundless capacity for self-deception, began to fail. He had lost a considerable part of his fortune in the enterprise, and he started selling parts of New Harmony to private individuals in the hope of recouping some of the losses. There were unpleasant lawsuits, and in July of 1827 Owen left New Harmony for good. Most of the inhabitants left shortly thereafter. Yet once away from the turmoil at New Harmony, Owen again began to tell lecture audiences about the marvelous success of the community, which, for all practical purposes, had already ceased to exist.

Because New Harmony had been the focus of so much attention, post mortems on its death have been endless. Many reasons have been offered for the failure. In fact, New Harmony didn't fail because it never was properly started. For all his business training Owen had no practical plan, only a dream. He had purchased the land with little fore-thought, then advertised for people to fill it. As a result he had to take what he got. The hundreds who arrived at New Harmony lacked a common background, common religion, shared ideas; they did not even have the same expectations about what the community was to become. Some had their own ideas, but most relied on Owen, and Owen didn't ever know.

BROOK FARM AND FRUITLANDS

Perhaps the most idyllic of all nineteenth century American communities was Brook Farm. It was located on a lush and beautiful site in Massachusetts near the Charles River, close enough to Boston so that it could easily be visited by wealthy and influential sympathizers. At least one of America's most prominent writers, Nathaniel Hawthorne, lived and worked at the community for a time. Another, Ralph Waldo Emerson, was well acquainted with it. Both have left behind accounts of life at Brook Farm, and although these accounts are not particularly flattering, they have made the community much more famous than some of its larger and more successful counterparts. But in the history of American communal movements, Brook Farm holds an honorable place.

The community was the brainchild of George Ripley, a

*Brook Farm in winter.* Top: *Original farm house, renamed "The Hive" by Brook Farmers, West Roxbury.* Bottom: *The Brook Bridges.*

Unitarian minister from Boston who had found the doctrines of his own church stifling. Ripley was part of a social group in which socialistic and liberal religious ideas were often discussed. By 1841 Ripley had tired of empty discussions and decided to do something. He resigned his ministry and set out to found a community. The first public announcement of Brook Farm came in an article entitled, "A Glimpse of Christ's Idea of Society." The article spoke in sweeping terms of establishing the Kingdom of God on earth—that kingdom in which "the will of God shall be done as it is done in heaven; a higher state than that of the apostolic church; worth even to be called the Second Coming of Christ; and the beginning of the Day of Judgement!"

In fact, this announcement was rather misleading, for the people who settled at Brook Farm were not confirmed millennialists, or even deeply religious in the way that the Shakers and the Rappites had been. They were, for the most part, Christians, but Christians attracted by the doctrine called Transcendentalism. Transcendentalism was a sort of humanist religion, though it was never formalized in any sense, and therefore the doctrine meant different things to different people. It became a religious or philosophical umbrella under which many liberal-minded Christians gathered. The Transcendentalists tried to open their system of belief to the science of the day, as well as to the ideas of non-Christian religions, particularly Oriental mysticism. Their only common belief was "in an order of truth that transcends the sphere of the external senses."

In addition to their spiritual aims, the intellectuals who came to Brook Farm had social aims. The leaders were well acquainted with Owen's theories and the Owenite experiments. Though they did not share Owen's agnosticism, they did share his faith in mankind's basic goodness, and ability to be transformed by his environment. On balance, it was probably the social and humanistic aims of the communards of Brook Farm, rather than their religious ideas, that provided the sustaining ideology for the community.

The economic organization of Brook Farm was fairly complicated. It was not a matter of everybody sharing everything. Members of the community bought stock in Brook Farm and were paid wages for their work by the community. From these wages they paid for food and other necessities of life; individuals who for health reasons were unable to work were supported by the community. However, these structures were less important than the genuine communal spirit that prevailed at the Farm.

As we have seen, most of the religious communities have been more or less ascetic and determinedly anti-intellectual. Such restrictions had no attraction for the middle-class intellectuals who came to Brook Farm. They placed a great value on leisure time. So great that Emerson derided the community as "a perpetual picnic." But leisure time to the Brook Farmers was to be a time in which they could improve their intellectual capacities. They hoped to be able to provide "not only all the necessaries, but all the elegances desirable for bodily and spiritual health; books, apparatus, collections for science, works of art, means of beautiful amusement," according to Elizabeth Palmer Peabody, who had also described the community as the Kingdom of God on this earth. No nineteenth century community pursued the intellectual and artistic life more vigorously than did Brook Farm.

But they also wished to be self-supporting, and to do that, hard physical labor was necessary. The Brook Farm intellectuals were not romantic about physical labor. Wrote Ripley, "We meant to lessen the labouring man's great burden of toil by performing our due share of it at the cost of our own thews and sinews." All labor, whether intellectual or physical, was to be rewarded by the community at the same rate, for if the labor was merely physical, "it is a greater sacrifice to the individual labourer to give his time to it; because time is desirable for the cultivation of the intellect, in exact proportion to ignorance. Besides, intellectual labour involves in itself higher pleasures, and is more its own reward, than bodily labour."

The sudden plunge from intellectual labor to bodily labor did not always proceed easily. Hawthorne reported that he got so tired working in the fields that he would often lie down under a haystack and pray that he would never rise again. The workers frequently switched from job to job to avoid boredom and were doubtless not the most efficient in the world.

Despite all this, for several years Brook Farm was a short-lived but real success. Writes Professor Mark Holloway, "They lived in an atmosphere that was enlivened by intellectual tolerance and free discussion; their nightly dances, their frequent picnics and boating parties, their performances of plays, their pageants, tableaux, and charades all testified to a free contentment that is rare among community members."

Yet there is an air of unreality about Brook Farm. It seems more like a pastoral gathering of Boston intellectuals than a genuine communitarian society. Starting with a mere twenty members, Brook Farm, for all its later fame, never had more than seventy members. This exclusive little community never wanted any more members.

Though the Brook Farmers did manage to support themselves, it was not from farming, a task for which they were poorly fitted. The bulk of the community's income came from an excellent school they had established.

Ultimately this pleasant little society was swept up and destroyed by a bizarre communitarian excitement called Fourierism, which will be discussed.

Bronson Alcott, a Boston teacher and Trancendentalist, had been invited to join Brook Farm, but he found the community too crude for his lofty ideals. Today Alcott might find a home at some of the more rigorous ecologically oriented communities. His main purpose in life was to leave the earth alone.

"The pure soul," he wrote, "by the law of its own nature, adopts a pure diet and cleanly customs; nor needs detailed rules for daily conduct. The greater part of man's duty consists in leaving alone much that he is in the habit of doing. . . . Shall I consume pork, beef or mutton? Not if you value health or life. . . . Shall I warm my bathing water? No, if purity is aimed at. Shall I prolong my dark hours, consuming animal oil, and losing bright daylight in the morning? Not if a clear mind is an object. Shall I teach my children the dogma inflicted on myself, under the pretense that I am transmitting truth? Nay, if you love them intrude not these between the Spirit of the Truth. Shall I become a hireling, or hire others? Shall I subjugate cattle? Shall I trade? Shall I claim property in any created things? Shall I adopt a form of religion? . . ." To all of those questions Bronson Alcott answered no. The language may be stilted, but the ideas are familiar to many communitarians today.

Alcott's list of abstentions was formidable, and to try to run a colony with such rules was risky, but try Alcott did. He was helped considerably by the financial backing of a rich English disciple. The community, situated near Harvard, Massachusetts, was called Fruitlands, primarily because of the strict vegetarian habits of the members. Alcott even refused to wear wool, because the sheep would feel the loss, or to use cotton, because it was produced by slave labor. It is difficult to imagine how such a community could have survived a New England winter. Fruitlands didn't. The community, begun in the spring of 1843, ended in the autumn of that very same year.

There were other small communities started at about the same time, like Hopedale and Skaneateles. But none was as successful as Brook Farm nor as exotic as Fruitlands, and all were soon swallowed up by the Fourier movement.

THE PHALANXES

The most extraordinary communitarian excitement to strike America during the nineteenth century was based upon the theories of a wildly eccentric Frenchman. There are undoubtedly more polite ways of describing Charles Fourier, but none would be more accurate.

Fourier was born in Paris in 1772. His father had been a wealthy merchant, and he was raised in the expectation that he would be comfortably supported for life. But the French Revolution intervened and wiped out the family fortune. Fourier was left with only a tiny legacy. For most of his life he lived alone in a series of dreary furnished rooms, befriended only by the cats that he loved. Perhaps to compensate for this melancholy existence, Fourier constructed, on paper, a perfect world—no, a perfect universe.

He described the life-span of the stars and how the moon had contracted a fever from the earth shortly before the Flood. He saw the earth passing through a myriad of periods and subperiods, including a period of Harmony, when the sea would turn to lemonade and all of the wild animals of the world would become lovable and tame. It was the ancient dream of the millennium, but infinitely more complex and fantastic.

Fourier, like Owen and many other social theorists, believed that God had made man good, and that it was a bad environment that turned him evil. Fourier therefore set about devising a perfect society, one that would not corrupt man's nature. He was a compulsive organizer, and his perfect society was divided into a bewildering number of divisions and subdivisions. At the base of his society was the Group, consisting of at least seven persons. The Group itself could be divided into two wings and a center, with at least two persons in each wing and three in the center. Each wing represented "ascending" and "descending" tastes and tendencies, and the center was to hold them in balance. The wings and the center were supposed to engage in healthy competition in whatever task was assigned to them, and that could be anything from garbage collecting to fruit tree growing. At least five Groups made up a Series, which also had its ascending and descending wings and its center. The Series were organized into a Phalanx, which was to contain between sixteen hundred and twenty and eighteen hundred members. The Phalanx was a complete and self-supporting unit, in which every individual should be able to find fulfillment.

Also like Owen, Fourier had an exact idea of what the physical arrangement of his perfect community should be. He never built a model, but probably would have if he had had the money. The site on which the Phalanx was to be located had to be at least three miles square. At its center was the Phalanstery, a vast building containing apartments, kitchens, schools, recreation rooms, and so forth. Naturally, the main portion of the building had two wings and a center. Granaries, stables, and other such work areas were housed in a long building attached to the main building, thus forming a hollow square. The interior of the square was a parade ground where each morning the various Groups and Series would gather under their special banners to march off to their appointed tasks.

Fourier filled his writings with descriptions of lavish feasts that were to be held as regular celebrations, and he devised a complicated and detailed system of sexual pairing. All this from a timid bachelor who existed on a near-starvation diet.

In retrospect, the works of Charles Fourier seem so absurd that it is hard to imagine that anyone could ever have taken them seriously, much less try to establish a community based upon them. Fourier himself never tried to found a Phalanx, and he disowned the one communitarian

*Charles Fourier, from an engraving made after a painting.*

experiment made in his name during his lifetime. Fourier waited in vain for some millionaire to finance a community on what he considered an appropriate scale. As a result, his ideas never had much impact in France, and when Charles Fourier died in 1837, he was virtually unknown in his native land.

But Fourier's doctrines attracted an enthusiastic and talented young American disciple named Albert Brisbane, who had been a student in France. Brisbane was considerably more level headed than his master, and when he returned to America to spread the gospel of Fourierism, he carefully left out all of the French philosopher's more far-fetched ideas. Brisbane concentrated on the formation of communities or, in Fourieristic jargon, Phalanxes or Associations.

The Association as envisioned by Brisbane was not total communism, any more than Brook Farm had been. Members and nonmembers alike were allowed to buy shares from which dividends were paid as soon as the community made a profit. The members of the various Groups and Series were paid wages according to a fixed scale. The highest wages were paid for the hardest and most disagreeable work. Each member purchased what he needed from the community and paid for his purchases from his wages. It all seemed very organized and practical, a perfect blending of ancient communal ideas and the new scientific method. If a Phalanx was constructed properly, Brisbane was convinced that total success was inevitable.

Brisbane's enthusiasm infected Horace Greeley, who was to become editor of the influential New York *Tribune*. Greeley gave Brisbane a regular column in the paper, and through it Fourier's ideas were spread far and wide. By 1840 an enthusiastic Fourieristic movement had developed in the United States. Ralph Waldo Emerson wrote to an English friend in 1840, "We are all a little wild here with numberless projects of social reform. Not a reading man but has a draft of a new community in his waistcoat pocket . . ."

Soon the American Associationists began to try practicing what they had been preaching. Fourier himself would never have approved of any of the experiments. He would have denounced them as too small, too poorly financed, and lacking in adequate planning, and he would have been quite right.

Other communal societies did not carry as heavy a theoretical burden as did the Fourierist Phalanxes. Other societies could experiment and improvise as they grew. The most successful of them, the Shaker societies, were almost accidental developments. But Fourier had insisted that his Phalanxes would fail unless they followed strict and, as it turned out, impossible rules. Fourier wanted to start with a membership of at least sixteen hundred, a large parcel of good land, an enormous amount of capital. Brisbane's expectations were more modest. He asked merely for a starting membership of four hundred and an initial capital of $400,000. Not one of the fifty or so Phalanxes that were started in America came anywhere near even Brisbane's recommendation.

Fourier put forth what he had believed to be a scientific and rational plan for reforming human society. Those who were attracted by his ideas also believed that they were being scientific and rational. As it turned out, they were the most innocent and impractical sort of enthusiasts. A writer in the Fourierist publication the *Phalanx* (July, 1844) gives this account of the failure of one of the communities:

"The original founders of this Association, no doubt actuated by good motives, but lacking discretion, held out such a brilliant prospect of comfort and pleasure in the very infancy of the movement, that hundreds, without any correct appreciation of the difficulties to be undergone by a pioneer band, rushed upon the ground, expecting at once to realize the heaven they so ardently desired, and which the eloquent words of the lecturers had warranted them to hope

*Design for a Fourierist Phalanstery that was never built, from a book by Albert Brisbane published in 1840.*

for. Thus, ignorant of Association, possessed, for the most part of little capital, without adequate shelter from the inclemency of the weather, or even a sufficient store of the most common articles of food, without plan, and I had almost said, without purpose, save to fly from the ills they had already experienced in civilization, they assembled together such elements of discord as naturally in a short time led to their dissolution."

To many, the failure of a Phalanx meant more than disappointment. There was much physical hardship, and most of those attracted to the movement were not frontiersmen. Starvation and disease were frequent in the communities before they broke up and the members fled back to the society that they had so recently tried to abandon. Many had lost considerable sums of money and their jobs in the attempt to form a community. Yet despite one horror story after another, and despite repeated warnings about overenthusiasm by Brisbane and some of the more moderate leaders, the movement continued to spawn a succession of ill-prepared communities.

Perhaps the best description of the state of mind of these Associationists was provided by John Humphrey Noyes, who was himself to lead a highly successful community in later years. Said Noyes:

"They comforted themselves with the thought that, they *must* succeed; they *will* succeed; they *are* succeeding! These words they say over and over to themselves, and shout them to the public. Still debt hangs over them. They get a subsidy from outside friends. But the deficit increases. Meanwhile disease persecutes them . . . they lie idle in their loose sheds . . . sweating and shivering in misery and despair. Human parasites gather about them like vultures scenting prey from afar. Their own passions torment them. They are cursed with suspicion and the evil eye. They quarrel about religion. They quarrel about their food. They dispute about carrying over their principles. Eight or ten families desert. The rest worry on through the long years. Foes watch them with cruel exultation. Friends shout to them, 'Hold on a little longer!' They hold on just as long as they can, insisting that they are successful, or are just going to be, till the last. Then comes the 'break up'; and who can tell the agonies of that great corporate death!

"See how pathetically these soldiers of despair with defeat in full view, offer themselves to other Associations, and take comfort in the assurance that God will not drive them from the earth! See how the heroes of the 'forlorn hope' after defeat has come turn again and reorganize, refusing to surrender!"

Of the many Phalanxes started during the 1840s, only three can be considered even partial successes. Of these the North American Phalanx located near Red Bank, New Jersey, lasted the longest, nearly twelve years. Most of the leaders of Fourierism in America, like Brisbane and Greeley, were involved in the founding of this community, and visited it frequently. It was to be a testing ground and showcase for Fourierist theories, though Fourier would have been horrified by its minuscule scale. Rather than the recommended sixteen hundred members or even the revised four hundred members, the North American Phalanx started with a mere eighty members and a tiny capital of $8,000. The small number of Associationists were nonetheless divided into Groups and Series and built themselves a three-story Phalanstery. The inhabitants of the North American Phalanx turned to farming and fruit growing with relish and considerable success. This was surprising because most of them had been city people. Financially the North American Phalanx prospered, and Fourierist journals were filled with glowing and doubtless exaggerated accounts of the wonderful life there. There was, however, one major shortcoming; the cultural life that was supposed to be a part of every Phalanx was badly neglected at North American, in the attempt to keep the Association financially sound.

The primary historian of the Fourierist experiments was an émigré Scotsman named A. J. MacDonald. He traveled from dying community to dying community, trying to figure out what had gone wrong with the dream. Those who met MacDonald called him the "sombre pilgrim" and assumed that he had become sad after encountering the wrecks of so many communities and the destruction of so many high hopes. But at the North American Phalanx the sombre pilgrim found a more cheerful scene. During a visit in July of 1852 MacDonald described the peculiar compulsiveness that seemed to infect the disciples of Charles Fourier. Whereas in most communities there was a minimum of record keeping and organization, it was very different at North American.

"They have altered their eating and drinking arrangements," wrote MacDonald, "and adopted the eating house system. At the table there is a bill of fare, and each individual calls for what he wants; on obtaining it the waiter gives him a check, with the price of the article marked thereon. After the meal is over, the waiters go round and enter the sum marked upon the check which each person has received, in a book belonging to that person; the total is added up at the end of each month and the payments are made. Each person finds his own sugar, which is kept upon the table. Coffee is half-a-cent per cup, including milk; bread one cent per plate; butter, I think, half-a-cent; meat two cents; pie two cents; and other things in like proportion. . . . In addition to this, as all persons use the room alike, each pays the same rent, which is thirty-six and a half cents per week; each person also pays a certain proportion for the waiting labor, for lighting the room. The young ladies and gentlemen who waited on the table, as well as the Phalanx Doctor . . . who from attraction performed the same duty, get six and a quarter cents per hour for their labor.

"The wages of various occupations, agricultural, mechanical and professional, vary from six cents to ten cents per hour; the latter sum is the maximum. The wages are paid to each individual in full every month, and the profits are divided at the end of the year. Persons wishing to become members are invited to become visitors for thirty days. At the end of that time it is sometimes necessary for them to continue another thirty days; then they may be admitted as probationers for one year. . . ."

MacDonald visited the North American Phalanx again in 1853, and found them still holding on. Yet the Associationists must certainly have felt a sense of discouragement. The North American was by that time the sole surviving Fourier Phalanx in the country. The movement that had begun with such wild enthusiasm in the 1840s was almost dead ten years later.

MacDonald himself died in 1854, and thus was spared witnessing the breakup of the final Phalanx. In 1854 there was a split within the North American, and a small group went off to form another short-lived community. In September a disastrous fire ate up all of the community's financial reserves. The crippled Phalanx limped on for yet another year, until its final dissolution.

A second partial success came in the Midwest. In 1844 a

small group of Associationists purchased a tract of cheap and poor land in the midst of an uninhabited prairie in Wisconsin. The leader of the group was a tough-minded organizer named Warren Chase, who kept almost unlimited control of the Phalanx from beginning to end. The Wisconsin Phalanx concentrated even more exclusively on making money than had the North American, and there was correspondingly less stress on cultural and educational achievements. Ultimately it seems that the Wisconsin Phalanx became so interested in making money that when their property became valuable in 1850 they sold it. The end of the Wisconsin Phalanx was not glorious, but it was the only Fourierist community that ever showed a profit.

While the Fourierist fever was raging, many of the members of Brook Farm became infected by it, and in 1844 that charming, though unreal community was transformed into The Brook Farm Phalanx. As a reward the Brook Farmers were treated to frequent visits and long, dull lectures from Albert Brisbane, Horace Greeley, and other Fourierist leaders. Brook Farm had a considerable reputation among American intellectuals at the time of its conversion to Fourierism, and it was a showplace for the movement. Brisbane and others used the community as a center for their propaganda. But somehow the spirit of Brook Farm was crushed by the weight of Fourierist theory. For two years the community labored to build a great Phalanstery, and when it was completed in 1846, it burned down almost immediately. The Brook Farmers had neither the financial resources nor the heart to rebuild, and within a year the community dissolved and the land was sold.

## ICARIA

Like Robert Owen and Charles Fourier, Étienne Cabet also dreamed of a perfect society. But instead of leading his followers to paradise, he led them through a series of disasters and hardships unparalleled in the history of American communities.

Cabet had been a revolutionary politician in France. In the turbulent era following the fall of Napoleon he had been in and out of the government. Finally he was exiled and spent time in England, where he became acquainted with Robert Owen and first encountered the work of his own countryman Charles Fourier.

When Cabet returned to France in 1839, he wrote a utopian novel called *A Voyage to Icaria*. As utopian books go, Cabet's work was tame and unoriginal, yet it enjoyed great success, and unexpectedly Cabet found himself the leader of a large socialist movement. He began looking for a spot to establish his Icaria. Owen was thinking about setting up a community in the new state of Texas, and he convinced Cabet that Texas was the promised land. A tricky Texas land agent sold the Frenchman a huge parcel of undeveloped property near the Red River. In 1848, amid great fanfare, a small advance party of Icarians set off for Texas, believing that a group of two thousand would be following shortly. Only after the party arrived in Texas did they realize that they had been cheated. The land of milk and honey they had expected turned out to be a desolate wilderness, and the conditions imposed upon the settlers by the land agents were so difficult as to make a successful community impossible. Yet they tried to stick it out. Several of the party died from exhaustion and disease, and the group's doctor went mad. Only the belief that very shortly two thousand new immigrants would arrive from France kept the survivors going. The following year a relief party did arrive; it consisted of ten exhausted and starving men.

Cabet was not insensitive to the sufferings of his followers. Mustering all his resources and influence, he gathered four hundred and fifty followers and about $17,000 and departed for America in 1849. Cabet did not make the mistake

*Étienne Cabet, from a contemporary print.*

of going to Texas. He took his followers to Nauvoo, Illinois, a town that had been built by the Mormons and then deserted by them in their trek westward. By that time the number of Cabet's followers had fallen to under three hundred, for some of the Icarians had become discouraged and others had been seduced away by good jobs with high wages in America.

At Nauvoo the Icarians enjoyed a brief period of prosperity. New arrivals swelled the ranks of the community to fifteen hundred. Most were hardworking French artisans whose talents were well appreciated in America. But the community began to chafe under Cabet's increasingly autocratic and unpredictable rule. He was over sixty at the time and becoming crotchety. Finally the community voted Cabet out of office, and in anger he led about one hundred and eighty of his closest followers to St. Louis. From there he tried to form another community, but his death in 1856 ended such efforts.

The Icarians at Nauvoo were dispirited after Cabet's departure, and many drifted away. The remaining members who held true to their original socialist faith moved to Iowa, where Nordhoff visited them in 1873. He found a poor community of only sixty-five members and called Icaria the "least prosperous of all the communities I have visited." He saw little hope for them and felt only pity for the sufferings they had endured.

From someone who knew of his visit, Nordhoff received a moving letter. "Please deal gently and cautiously with Icaria. The man who sees only the chaotic village and the wooden shoes, and only chronicles those, will commit a serious error. In that village are buried fortunes, noble hopes, and the aspirations of good and great men like Cabet. Fertilized by these deaths, a great and beneficent growth yet awaits Icaria. It has eventful and extremely interesting history, but its future is destined to be still more interesting.

It, and it alone, represents in America a great idea—rational democratic communism."

There was no great future for Icaria as the letter writer had predicted. It is surprising that there was any future at all. In 1873 the community seemed near death, yet so powerful was the Icarian dream that it persisted for over twenty more years. In 1883 the Icarians split, some moving to California, where their attempts to found a new community failed. The remainder lived on the old Icarian land, amid as much prosperity as they had ever known. The community was unable to hold its younger members and made no attempt to recruit new ones. By 1891 there were a mere twenty-one Icarians left, and they voted to end the community and divide the land privately among the survivors.

# 6  Oneida

John Humphrey Noyes was an American original. His mere existence is improbable, his success utterly fantastic. In the middle of the nineteenth century, while Victorian prudery set the moral tone for the United States, Noyes established a community where sexuality was encouraged and monogamy forbidden. Celibate societies might be tolerated, but the life-style that Noyes advocated so loudly and practiced so openly would be considered radical and dangerous even in our current permissive society. The wonder is that he was never hung.

Unlike the founders of most successful communities, John Humphrey Noyes came from a prosperous and socially prominent family. His father, a moderately wealthy businessman, had represented Vermont in Congress; his mother was a great-aunt of Rutherford B. Hayes, nineteenth President of the United States. Noyes was born in Brattleboro, Vermont, in 1811. Until the age of twenty he showed little interest in religion, but in 1831 he was swept up in the wave of religious excitement called the Great Revival. He left law school, which he hadn't much cared for anyway, and entered divinity school first at Andover and then at Yale.

"If you are to be a minister," his father warned, "you must think and preach as the rest of the ministers do; if you get out of the traces, they will whip you in."

"Never!" answered Noyes. "Never will I be whipped by ministers or anybody else into views that do not commend themselves to my understanding as guided by the Bible and enlightened by the Spirit." A bold statement, and as it turned out, a correct one.

Most of those saved during revivals were driven by a deep sense of personal sin. Here too Noyes was an original—try as he might, he just didn't feel like a sinner. But how could any mortal man be sinless? Basic Puritan doctrine held that man was totally depraved and could be saved only through God's grace. The problem seemed unresolvable in Christian terms, and no matter how unorthodox Noyes might have been, he always remained a devout Christian.

In the summer of 1833 Noyes received an illumination that resolved his difficulty completely. He felt sinless because he had already been saved. When reading the last words of the Fourth Gospel, Noyes saw what he believed to be the meaning behind Christ's words: "If I will that he tarry till I come, what is that to thee." Wrote Noyes, "I knew that the time appointed for the Second Advent was within one generation from the time of Christ's personal ministry." He fixed the date at A.D. 70. This interpretation of scripture, while unusual, was not totally unique. What was unique was the use to which Noyes put the belief. If Christ had already returned, he reasoned, then man could be made perfect on the earth. Noyes declared that he was perfect. Many of his friends and relatives thought he had gone mad. He was expelled from Yale, and his license to preach was revoked.

Moreover, though he was not a strict millennialist, Noyes was a firm believer in the possibility of establishing a "Kingdom of Heaven on earth." This Kingdom of Heaven was to be ruled by Biblical principles, as interpreted by John Humphrey Noyes, not by the rules of the rest of the world. The followers of Noyes' doctrine called themselves Perfectionists—not that they all believed themselves to be perfect, but they were striving toward that goal, and they felt that spiritual perfection was obtainable on this earth. There had been perfectionists before, but Noyes was the greatest of them.

The heaven on earth that Noyes sought was clearly to be a communal society. That was a conclusion that many before him had come to. But to Noyes, communism was only a secondary goal; his primary goal was far more radical. In a letter to a Perfectionist journal, *The Battle Axe*, Noyes explained that if earth was to become like heaven, then *"there will be no marriage. The marriage supper of the Lamb is a feast at which every dish is free to every guest. Exclusiveness, jealousy, quarrelling have no place there, for the same reason as that which forbids a guest at a thanksgiving dinner to claim each his separate dish, and quarrel with the rest for his rights. In a holy community, there is no more reason why sexual intercourse should be restrained by law, than why eating and drinking should be—and there is as little occasion for shame in one case as in the other."*

Later, as Noyes became more interested in the problems of a communal society, he advanced another reason for abandoning monogamy. Conventional marriage, he said, was utterly incompatible with the communal mode of life. It introduced ideas of exclusivity and selfishness that would ultimately destroy any communal society. Marriage, in his view, was nothing more than the exclusive possession of one person by another. To back up his argument, he pointed to the history of American communal societies; only the celibate groups like the Shakers and Rappites had any long-term success. But getting rid of marriage through celibacy

Noyes found both unnatural and unnecessary. For his heaven on earth, Noyes developed the idea of Complex Marriage, really a sort of regulated promiscuity.

In 1834 Noyes returned to his family home in Putney, Vermont, and began to build the nucleus of followers who were to make up his community. Among those who came under his influence was Harriet Holton, the granddaughter of a lieutenant governor of Vermont, an heiress whose money helped to support many of Noyes' early projects. In 1838 Noyes married her, despite his dislike of the institution of marriage. Noyes and his friends founded a small publication, *The Witness,* which was mailed to sympathetic individuals throughout the country. He might simply have been regarded as another New England eccentric, if he had not tried to put his heaven on earth into practical operation.

The idea of actually founding a Perfectionist society seemed to grow slowly. Noyes and his followers had no formal organization until 1840, when they organized the Putney Association. It was to be a strictly religious body. Said *The Witness,* "We are attempting no scientific experiments in political economy nor in social science, and we beg to be excused from association in the public mind with those who are making such experiments."

Four years later, however, the Perfectionists did begin an experiment in "political economy" by establishing a communal society on five hundred acres of fertile land near Putney. The first community was made up of forty to fifty people. Noyes was well known, and his community seemed eccentric but inoffensive, at first. Two years later the Putney Association openly and aggressively adopted the practice of Complex Marriage. That was too much for the neighbors. They began to harass Noyes and his followers, and ultimately Noyes was arrested for adultery.

Unlike Mother Ann, who seemed to relish imprisonment and martyrdom, Noyes had no taste for prison and no desire to be chased by howling mobs, so he jumped bail. He decided to abandon Vermont and purchased a tract of land on Oneida Creek halfway between Syracuse and Utica, New York. The land was excellent, and Noyes was a good businessman who had more financial resources at his command than the usual communitarian leader. Another valuable feature of Oneida was that it was located in the midst of what was called the Burned Over District. The region had obtained this name because it had been swept by the fires of repeated religious revivals. So many odd sects, including pre-Noyesan perfectionists, had developed there that the residents were relatively tolerant, even of Complex Marriage. Many of those who joined the Oneida community were residents of the Burned Over District.

Noyes' enemies pictured him as an unbridled sensualist, and the Oneida community as a hotbed of lust and free love. The picture was quite false. Noyes may have been a highly sexed man, but he also was an orderly, almost fussy one. He was motivated by what he saw as entirely rational and moral feelings, rather than by sensuality and emotion. Sex as practiced in conventional society just didn't make any sense to him. By selective interpretation of the Bible, he decided that society's view of sex had also been condemned by Christ and the Apostles.

Mother Ann of the Shakers had seen sexual relations as the cause of the Fall of man. John Humphrey Noyes saw the problem the other way around. He wrote:

"Adam and Eve were, at the beginning in open, fearless, spiritual fellowship, first with God, and secondly with each other. Their transgression produced two corresponding alienations, vis., first an alienation from God, indicated by their fear of meeting him and their hiding themselves among the trees of the garden; and secondly, an alienation from each other, indicated by their shame at their nakedness and their hiding themselves from each other by clothing." To

Noyes, reestablishing the proper relations between the sexes was second only to reestablishing the proper relations between man and God.

Traditional Christian doctrine held that sexual pleasure was merely bait for the true function of sex, which was procreation. Not so, said Noyes. Of the two functions, amativeness, or love, was the most important, and child rearing secondary. The Perfectionists were also great believers in population limitation. Noyes observed that childbearing was dangerous for women, and the raising of children burdensome for men. He had nothing against children *per se;* it was the idea of too many children that repelled him.

The dangers and heartbreak of childbearing were very personal to Noyes, for his own wife had given birth to five babies in six years, four of them born dead. He saw no reason for any woman to repeat such an experience. On the other hand, he did not approve of contraceptives. What he practiced, and recommended to others, was self-control, or *coitus reservatus.* Noyes called his system Male Continence, and he wrote endlessly on the subject, eventually making it one of the basic tenets of his community. All male members of Oneida were carefully instructed in Male Continence, and it worked quite well.

In theory any member of the Perfectionist community might have intercourse with any other member of the community of the opposite sex, providing that both agreed. In practice, however, things did not work out that way, for relations between the sexes, and all other personal relationships at Oneida, were regulated by various committees and another of Noyes' inventions, Mutual Criticism.

Any member of the community who felt guilty about something, or who was believed to be guilty of some error or personal failing, could be subjected to public criticism. He would come before the entire society or, more commonly, before a smaller group of persons who knew him best. Then all of those present would recount the "victim's" faults with

*John Humphrey Noyes.*

frankness, even brutality. But there was to be no hint of personal ill feeling or spitefulness. If this was detected, the critic would himself become the subject of criticism. The result of Mutual Criticism was to get deviates to conform to the standards of the group. Public discussion of individual sins was a common technique of social control in religious societies, but no society had ever depended so heavily upon this sort of activity. Today a form of Mutual Criticism, under the name group therapy, is commonly employed by psychiatrists. It is also used in some rehabilitation centers, like the drug rehabilitation community of Synanon.

The Perfectionists also believed that criticism could have medical as well as social benefits. Any sick member of the Oneida community, no matter what his ailment, was encouraged to seek criticism in the belief that a good critical session could cure practically anything. In cases where ailments were psychologically based, the criticism often did help, but whether such sessions generally improved the health of the community is unknown.

Primarily, though, Mutual Criticism was used to regulate social relationships. The community actively discouraged "selfish" mutual attachments of one person for another, and encouraged relationships that might not otherwise have developed. The Perfectionists consistently urged the young of one sex to pair off with the old of the other sex. "Even elderly people, whose physical passions had burned low, preserved the fine essence of earlier associations," wrote one of Noyes' sons.

The rather unemotional, even cold quality of personal life at Oneida is reflected in an experiment in scientific breeding, or eugenics, that the community embarked upon. Noyes, who enjoyed making up labels, called this experiment "stirpiculture." Some one hundred men and women, chosen for their physical and mental characteristics, were paired off, for the purpose of producing superior children. Fifty-eight children resulted from the experiment. Most observers agree that these children, and their children, constitute a very superior group—handsome, intelligent, and unusually healthy. Noyes, by the way, fathered ten of the stirpiculture children, whereas most of the other men fathered only one. This may have created some hard feelings in the community.

Oneida presents a paradox. To some (usually those who had never visited the place), it seemed a collection of lustful debauchees; to others, a group of cold and mechanical individuals, who ignored the laws of God and the finer instincts of man. But whatever outsiders thought of Oneida, the community itself got on remarkably well for a long time. By no stretch of the imagination could the Perfectionists be considered mad, and even the label fanatics is out of place. They were an orderly, commonsensical people, who had the courage to live in defiance of accepted standards. Most were New England farmers and mechanics, but there was a sprinkling of professional people like lawyers, physicians, and teachers.

When Oneida began, the accommodations were primitive, and for many years life there was physically hard. But the Oneida citizens were hard workers, and they were lucky. One of the early converts was an inventor named Sewell Newhouse, who had designed a superior steel animal trap and donated all proceeds from his invention to Oneida. The community members themselves began to manufacture the trap, and the profits from its sale carried them through the first few difficult years. Newhouse traps remained one of their most successful manufactured items. (It is ironic that such a generally kindly society should depend for its success on such a cruel device. One can hardly imagine the Shakers manufacturing animal traps.)

Although most communal societies were based on agriculture, the Perfectionists engaged in manufacturing as well. Gradually goods made at Oneida acquired a reputation for excellent workmanship, and sales of many items from preserved fruit to silk brought in handsome returns. As wealth grew, the community acquired more land and more members. By the early 1870s there were nearly three hundred Perfectionists. The bulk lived at Oneida, but smaller communities were also established; of these, only the branch at Wallingford, Connecticut, ever amounted to anything. Oneida and Wallingford essentially operated as a single unit with individuals traveling freely between them, as their skills were needed or as their desires moved them.

In 1848 the people at Oneida were housed in a few log cabins that had been on the land when it was first purchased. Over the years a variety of makeshift residences were constructed. In the early 1860s a huge brick hotellike structure called the Mansion House was built. The building was large enough to house all those at the community with the exception of ten or twenty workmen who lived closer to their shops about a mile away.

When compared to the early days at Oneida, indeed when compared to the residence of the average workingman of the day, the Mansion House was truly a mansion. It was centrally heated and well supplied with indoor plumbing and ingenious laborsaving devices. The younger members of the community slept in double bedrooms, while the older ones had rooms to themselves, if they desired. There were visitors' rooms, recreation rooms, and a large library containing over five thousand volumes.

Most religious communities feared or at least disliked the literature of the world and limited themselves to reading the Bible and selected religious books, usually those written by the founder of the sect. Not so the Perfectionists. No idea was forbidden to them, and they positively embraced the world's knowledge, particularly in the area of science. Even the works of Darwin and Huxley, which were still an anathema to the majority of devout Christians in America, could be found on the shelves of the library at Oneida.

Music and dancing, card games, plays, and other frivolities that were damned by the Puritans were welcomed by their Perfectionist descendants. Once the Perfectionists became prosperous, they did their best to beautify their community. Oneida even owned a couple of summer resorts on lakes and at the ocean, where members might enjoy cooling breezes and refreshing swims during the hot months.

Oneida seemed to get along quite well without the rigid rules that governed the Shakers and other successful communities. The Perfectionists seemed to have a genuine horror of scheduling. The hours of meetings and meals, even the number of meals eaten daily, were changed frequently just to avoid routine. There was no particular time for members to arise in the morning, nor were jobs and hours of work assigned. Jobs were changed often to ward off boredom, and dull or disagreeable jobs were changed more frequently than satisfying ones. But from all accounts there was little shirking of necessary work.

If Oneida was to be heaven on earth, the residents should not have to work so hard that they would have no time for other things in life. So the community was forced to hire outside labor. It hired a higher percentage of outside labor than any other American communal society. The community members usually served as supervisors while the hired help did the dirty work. The hired laborers rarely complained, for they were well paid and well treated. The high wages paid by Oneida is one of the reasons the unorthodox community was generally popular with its neighbors. But Noyes had never meant that his community should become a benevolent oligarchy. He hoped that one day it would grow so large that the need for hired labor would disappear. That hope never came to pass.

In no society, including the Shakers, was there as much equality between the sexes as at Oneida. Among the Shakers women still did the traditional women's work, but at Oneida women were trained as mechanics or blacksmiths, if that was what they wanted. A woman was head bookkeeper at

Oneida, and the system she devised was praised by outsiders as a marvel of efficiency and precision. Women also served on all important committees and were entirely equal in the decision-making process—at least in theory. In fact, it was Noyes who made most of the important decisions.

For women to share equally in the work, they had to be relieved of the duties of child raising. Children born at Oneida stayed with their mothers until they were weaned, and then were placed in a nursery to be raised by the community as a whole. Although children were not encouraged to reject their parents, they were told not to regard them as anyone special. Outsiders found the nursery a rather cheerless place. One compared the Oneida children to "a lot of little chickens raised in an egg-hatching machine, and having a blanket for shelter instead of the wing of a mother." It wasn't all that bad. In reminiscences about their childhood some who had grown up at Oneida complained that as children they felt lonely and somewhat neglected. But, in general, they had happy memories, and there is no indication that they were in any way harmed by being raised communally. Still, it seems fair to conclude that children fared less well at Oneida than did adults.

Noyes was a great believer in the power of printed propaganda, but he never minced words, no matter what effect they might have on his readers. The fullest and frankest expression of his views came in a book entitled *Bible Communism*—the title is a little more loaded now than when Noyes wrote it, but the contents certainly are not. Of monogamy he said:

"(It) gives to sexual appetite only a scanty and monotonous allowance and so produces the natural vices of poverty, contraction of taste and stinginess or jealousy. It makes no provision for the sexual appetite at the very time when that appetite is the strongest. By the custom of the world, marriage in the average of cases, takes place at about the age of twenty-four; whereas puberty commences at the age of fourteen. For ten years, therefore, and in the very flush of life, the sexual appetite is starved. This law of society bears hardest on females, because they have less opportunity of choosing their time of marriage than men."

The most effective vehicle of Noyesan propaganda was a well-written weekly paper, the *Circular*, published at Oneida. Noyes was determined to get his paper into the hands of any interested party, no matter what the cost. The means of subscription was highly unusual:

"The *Circular* is sent to all applicants, whether they pay or not. It costs and is worth at least two dollars per volume. Those who want it and ought to have it are divisible into three classes, vis: 1, those who can not afford to pay two dollars; 2, those who can afford to pay *only* two dollars; and 3, those who can afford to pay *more* than two dollars. The first ought to have it free; the second ought to pay the cost of it; and the third ought to pay enough more than the cost to make up the deficiencies of the first. This is the law of Communism. We have no means of enforcing it, and no wish to do so, except by stating it and leaving it to the good sense of those concerned. We take the risk of offering the *Circular* to all without price. . . ."

Not surprisingly, the *Circular* regularly lost money.

Unlike most zealots, the Perfectionists had some sense of humor about their endeavor, as these "advertisements" printed in the *Circular* indicate:

TO JEWELERS.—A SINGLE PEARL OF GREAT PRICE! This inestimable Jewel may be obtained by application to Jesus Christ, at the extremely low price of "all that a man hath!"

### TO BROKERS.
WANTED.—Any amount of SHARES OF SECOND-COMING STOCK, bearing date A.D. 70, or thereabouts, will find a ready market and command a high premium at this office.

D IRECTIONS for cultivating the fruits of the Spirit may
    be obtained *gratis*, at        MEEK & LOWLY'S,
                                         No. 1 Grace Court.

The journalist Charles Nordhoff visited Oneida in 1873 when the society was at its height. He was impressed by what he saw and tried to be sympathetic. But he found much of Oneida life jarring. Nordhoff felt more comfortable with the celibate Shakers and Rappites. He wrote:

"The men dress as people of the world do, but plainly each following his own fancy. The women wear a dress consisting of bodice, loose trousers, and a short skirt falling to just above the knee. Their hair is cut just below the ears, and I noticed that the younger women usually give it a curl. The dress is no doubt extremely convenient; it admits of walking in mud or snow, and allows freedom of exercise; and it is entirely modest. But it was to my unaccustomed eyes totally and fatally lacking in grace and beauty." The women's outfit was designed by Noyes.

The proper mode of address in this world of Complex Marriage was bound to be something of a problem. The men were called "mister" and the women "miss" except those who had been married before coming to Oneida. Nordhoff found it "somewhat startling to hear Miss _____ speak about her baby."

Nordhoff praised the ingenuity, industriousness, and organizational abilities of the Perfectionists. But what most fascinated him, and everybody since, was their social relations, particularly their sexual relations. Nordhoff was invited to attend one of the Sunday Mutual Criticism sessions. In this session the object of criticism was a young man Nordhoff called Charles, who had offered himself for criticism because he felt a lack of faith and a falling away from religion. About fifteen people, including Noyes, attended the session. Noyes did not lead the criticism; for the most part he sat in a large rocker and listened attentively.

For about half an hour Charles was subjected to a barrage of criticism from the group. One said he was spoiled, another that he was careless with language, another that he complained about the food and had bad table manners, and so on. One of his defenders said that Charles was a good fellow, but that he really had no religion at all.

No one held back any complaint. Said Nordhoff, "The people knew very well how to express themselves. There was no vagueness, no uncertainty. Every point was made; every sentence was a hit—a stab I was going to say, but as the sufferer was a volunteer, I suppose that would be too strong a word."

Volunteer or not, this session of criticism was clearly painful. "Charles sat speechless, looking before him; but as the accusations multiplied, his face grew paler, and drops of perspiration began to stand on his forehead."

It fell to Noyes to sum up the criticism. He said that although Charles did have serious faults he seemed to be a person of basically good character who was making strenuous efforts to correct himself. Noyes then reported that Charles had recently come to him with a problem concerning one of Noyes' favorite themes. "In the course of what we call stirpiculture, Charles, as you know, is in the situation of one who is by and by to become a father. Under these circumstances, he has fallen under the too-common temptation to selfish love, and a desire to wait upon and cultivate an exclusive intimacy with the woman who was to bear a child through him. This is an insidious temptation, very apt to attack people under such circumstances; but it must nevertheless be struggled against." Noyes was very heartened to find that Charles had succeeded in fighting off his desire for exclusivity.

That was too much for the conventional Nordhoff. He admitted that the criticism might have been beneficial to Charles, and that it was probably also beneficial to the critics, for it dissipated any bitterness they might hold. But,

*Perfectionists in front of one wing of the Oneida Mansion House in 1867.*

"Concerning the closing remarks of Noyes, which disclose so strange and horrible a view of morals and duty, I need say nothing."

Strange and horrible it may have been to Nordhoff, but it worked. Very few of the young people left the society, and many who did leave tried to return. Only one person had been expelled from Oneida up to the time Nordhoff visited. Oneida was extremely careful about accepting new members, and there were always plenty of applications. All the

Perfectionists that Nordhoff interviewed seemed happy and satisfied with their way of life, even a bit smug about it. The community's neighbors regarded the Perfectionists as industrious and honest folk, and didn't bother much about their unusual living arrangements.

But the apparent stability Nordhoff saw was illusion. Three years after his visit Noyes fled the community, and by 1879 most of the basic principles upon which Oneida was founded had been abandoned. What had happened?

Superficially it was the sustained attacks of Professor John W. Mears of Hamilton College that forced Noyes to flee. Mears was enraged by what he called Oneida's "ethics of the barnyard." Complex Marriage was clearly illegal, and if the complaints against the Perfectionists were brought into court, Noyes might well have wound up in jail. Noyes had evidence that a number of members of the community were getting ready to support Professor Mears, so on June 23, 1876, he suddenly and secretly crossed the border into Canada at Niagara Falls. He never returned to the United States.

There was nothing new or startling in the Mears attack. All the charges had been made before, and the Perfectionists had rallied solidly behind their leader to defeat their enemies. But discontent within the community was rising as a new generation born and raised at Oneida grew up and assumed power.

For all their unorthodoxy, Noyes' original followers were devoted Christians. It was the deep religious conviction that they were God's people that had sustained them through all the hardships and hostility. Noyes constantly stressed the need for religion in a successful community. But the younger generation lacked the religious fervor of their elders. Indeed, many were not Christians at all. When Noyes tried to retire from active leadership in 1876 and turn the community over to his son Dr. Theodore Noyes, this subterranean conflict broke into the open. The younger Noyes was an outspoken agnostic, and he lacked his father's ability to inspire devotion. Noyes was compelled to come out of retirement and take over the community again, but it was too late. Noyes was no coward, but he was a pragmatist with no taste for martyrdom, especially in his old age. He abandoned the battle.

Even from Canada, Noyes' influence on Oneida remained supreme. In 1879 he sent a letter to the community advising them to give up the practice of Complex Marriage, "not as renouncing belief in the principles and prospective finality of that institution, but in deference to the public sentiment which is evidently rising against it." He recommended adopting Saint Paul's view, which "allows marriage but prefers celibacy." The Oneida community quickly accepted the suggestion. But most of the community members preferred marriage to celibacy, and a considerable number of marriages were hastily performed.

By 1881 the communal ownership of goods was abandoned, and Oneida was reorganized as a joint stock company called Oneida Community Limited. The financial settlement was wise and just, and very few complained about it. The company has prospered, and today it is a model corporation in which owners and workers share the profits. Oneida is the largest producer of stainless steel tableware and the second largest producer of silverplated tableware in the United States. It is a multimillion-dollar operation with plants in Canada, Mexico, and Great Britain. After making the switch from communism to capitalism, the community itself began to break up. People moved out of the Mansion House into separate dwellings. Others left the area entirely, fifty or so going to Canada to be near their exiled leader. These were the old guard, and Noyes had to dissuade them from trying to set up another colony along the lines of the original Oneida.

Most of the descendants of the Oneida experiment, however, still live in the vicinity of Oneida, some in the old Mansion House itself. They take considerable pride in the daring of their nineteenth century ancestors, particularly in Noyes, or the Honorable John, as they call him. But there seems no general movement to repeat the experiment in this century.

Noyes died in April of 1886. To the end he remained confident and undiscouraged. He had good reason to be pleased —his community had flourished for over a quarter of a century, an enviable record. The principles upon which Oneida had been established were to Noyes absolutely correct. The breakup of the community did not shake his faith; it simply seemed that the time for such a society had not yet arrived. Noyes was a great believer in cycles and proper timing. Given the communitarian excitement that grips America today, John Humphrey Noyes might well feel that a time for a new Oneida was at hand.

# 7 🌿 The New Millennium?

John Humphrey Noyes saw two movements as leading to the growth of communes during the nineteenth century—revivalism and socialism. "Both failed in their attempts to bring heaven on earth," he wrote, "*because* they despised each other, and would not put their two great ideas together. The Revivalists failed for want of regeneration of society, and the Socialists failed for want of regeneration of heart."

By the end of the nineteenth century both of these two movements had become hostile to the founding of new communes. Revivals were by then financed primarily by businessmen. Revivalists loyally supported the interests of their patrons by preaching that Christ and the free enterprise system were allies. The good Christian, to the late nineteenth and early twentieth century revivalists, was supposed to oppose experimentation with any "foreign" or "socialistic" ideas. Not only were such ideas foolish, they claimed, but they also were inspired by the Devil himself. Similarly, evangelist Billy Graham is no friend of the modern commune movement.

The socialist movement of the early 1900s, on the other hand, had fallen largely under the influence of Karl Marx and his disciples. To Marxist socialists, utopian socialists like Robert Owen were hopelessly unrealistic and potentially dangerous, for they diverted people's energies from the real struggle for "scientific" socialism. In place of the nineteenth century socialist's faith in the innate goodness of man, and the possibility of changing society by example and evolution, came the Marxist view of class struggle and revolution. In surviving communities like Icaria, where socialist ideas had been strong, many of the young took to Marxism and abandoned the commune.

Aside from changes in religion and political ideology, some hard economic facts contributed to the decline of the nineteenth century communitarian movement. For a long time well-run communities had been able to compete successfully with the rest of society. Shakers, Rappites, Perfectionists, and Inspirationists, all lived more comfortable and secure lives than they could reasonably have expected in the world at large. Even uninspiring and mediocre communities like Dr. Keil's Bethel and Aurora gave their members a measure of security and comfort not found among their noncommunal neighbors.

Today the commune can no longer compete on the economic front. The most successful modern communal society, the Hutterites, has managed to thrive only by hard work and plain living. And for all their success the Hutterites are really no more prosperous than their neighbors.

Most of the early American communes were made up of immigrants seeking a place in the vast American wilderness where they would be left alone. Both distance and differences in custom and language helped to isolate these communities from the outside world. By the end of the nineteenth century the wilderness had largely disappeared. The mass immigrations stopped in the early years of the twentieth century. America today is a vastly different land from the one to which Ann Lee and George Rapp had led their followers.

Communes continued to exist throughout the first half of the twentieth century, just as they had for more than two centuries. Some were odd and colorful, but none were very successful. Communes in other countries, particularly the kibbutzim of Israel, attracted some attention, but few believed that their model could be successfully transferred to the American scene. The idea that there was any sort of a commune movement in America was dead by the end of the nineteenth century. Then late in the 1960s America suddenly rediscovered the commune.

When did this new movement begin? How large is it? What are the social, ideological, or religious ideas behind it? What does it mean to traditional American values? Is the commune movement really a movement at all? All of these questions and many others have been asked over and over again. Unfortunately, there are no really satisfactory answers, because the modern commune movement is too amorphous to generalize about without distorting the picture.

Take the question of the size of the movement—how many communes are there in America today? Estimates vary—one thousand, two thousand, three thousand; these figures are little more than wild guesses. Since there has been no census of communes, nobody really knows the extent of the movement. Besides, many modern communes are extremely unstable, and no census would be accurate for very long. The number of rural communes, particularly in the Northeast, drops sharply during the winter and rises again when warm weather comes.

There is even a problem of definition; what is a commune? One writer called it "any arrangement of three or more persons whose primary bond is some form of common sharing, rather than blood or legal ties." A half dozen people sharing the rent on a large apartment and splitting the cooking and

*Many young communalists have rejected modern urban life for the simpler life of early rural America.*

cleaning duties might call themselves a commune. In another time they might have called themselves roommates.

Most of the people who live in communes now seem to believe that they are involved in some sort of movement, but it is a movement that has no organization, no leadership, and few clear shared goals.

As we pointed out, communes have been around almost continuously since America began. An early prophet of the current communal, back-to-the-land movement was Peter Maurin, a French Catholic émigré, who preached what he called the Green Revolution. Maurin saw a cure for many of society's ills in a return to simple farming. Today, many who have never heard of Peter Maurin or his Green Revolution have reached the same conclusion. Maurin joined up with Dorothy Day, an ex-communist turned radical Catholic, and together they founded the Catholic Worker Movement during the Great Depression of the 1930s.

There never have been a great number directly involved in the Catholic Workers, but the moral influence of its two remarkable founders has been far more widespread than one might imagine. Although most of the movement's work has been carried on in the cities among the urban poor, the Catholic Workers have never given up Peter Maurin's dream of a return to the land.

In the 1930s a string of Catholic Worker communal farms was established. William D. Miller, author of a recent biography of Dorothy Day, points out that the farms attracted not only a considerable number of radical Catholics, but some cranks as well:

"It was an unusual group at the farm that summer—a circumstance that for the Catholic Worker was completely usual. There was a man just out of Sing Sing who planted flowers, a seminarian who brought six pigs . . . and an ex-circus performer who would do cartwheels down the hill in back of the house when the moon was full."

At another farm he noted:

"A cabal developed against Dorothy Day, the leader of which was the head of one family that lived on the upper farm. . . . Emphasizing 'the priesthood of the laity,' he gathered about him a group of which his family was the center. This man designated one of the group its 'spiritual adviser' and then proceeded to bedeck his person with symbols of authority, insisting on the performance of solemn obeisances from the others—bowing, kneeling, and the like—and when they ran afoul of his edicts, penances were imposed. . . . The women were forbidden to speak unless spoken to and were compelled to knock on the doors of even their own kitchens if men were present."

In the 1960s many middle-class hippies were attracted to Catholic Worker farms, but their drugs and sexual promiscuity were too much for Dorothy Day, who despite all her radicalism remains a devoutly religious Catholic. She denounced their life-style as "a complete rebellion against authority, natural and supernatural, even against the body and its needs, its natural functions of childbearing. . . ."

Today the major remaining Catholic Worker farm is Tivoli Farm on Staten Island. When the Catholic Workers bought the farm, the area was largely rural. Though the farm continues to exist, the pressures on it and all other farms on increasingly urbanized Staten Island grow daily.

The farm has only a small permanent membership, but many others from the Catholic Worker center in New York City, as well as casual visitors, spend time there. Often they find that farm work, hard as it is, is a relief after the pressures of city life. Those who stay at the farm, like those in the Catholic Worker center in the city, are a mixture of middle-class idealists and former derelicts. The rules, though not strict and only informally enforced, do not tolerate the "do your own thing" attitude that the public has come to associate with modern communes.

Forming a radical, interracial commune in the middle of Georgia's Ku Klux Klan country in 1942 might seem an impossible, even suicidal, undertaking. Yet that is exactly what Clarence Jordan did. Jordan, a Ph.D. in theology, dreamed of a place where poor whites and poor blacks could farm together in dignity and equality. He called his farm Koinonia, which comes from a Greek word meaning "fellowship" or "community." With very little capital, but great determination and courage, Jordan and some associates started their farm near Americus, Georgia, not far from the site of the infamous Civil War prison camp of Andersonville. The Koinonia community has endured boycotts, threats, beatings, and shootings. Today it is reasonably secure and more prosperous than it has ever been. Koinonia faces an unexpected new threat, however, from militant blacks who dislike its efforts at integration and denounce the farm's Christianity as the "white man's religion."

The Koinonia community is not large. It has never had more than thirty or forty full-time residents. But during summers college students from all parts of the country come to help out. And many people involved in radical, nonviolent politics or radical Christianity have at least heard of the experiment. For communitarians who know the history of their movement, Koinonia is a sort of shrine.

Jordan had hoped that his community would serve as a model and an inspiration for others. In language worthy of an old-time Anabaptist, he wrote:

"The sowing of the seed, the spread of the radical ideas of the gospel message. . . . It means to preach news to the poor, to proclaim release to the captives and recovering of sight to the blind, to set at liberty those who are oppressed, to proclaim the acceptable year of the Lord."

Jordan died in 1969. His experiment had not inspired any imitators as he had hoped. Two days before his death he wrote:

"We have sought out dedicated people to share the dream and to be partners. Materialism, competitiveness, and self-interest are so deeply entrenched in our culture that they have almost exterminated the spirit of partnership and sharing. But people with this spirit have been coming. Many more are needed, but we have faith that, in time, they will come. The breed is not yet extinct."

It was not courageous experiments like Tivoli Farm and Koinonia, however, that focused public attention on the commune once again; rather it was the development of hip communes, primarily on the West Coast during the late 1960s. The dream of peace and love pursued by the generation of the "flower children" had turned into a nightmare.

*At Drop City, inexpensive adobe was the basic building material. Modern lightweight domes were sometimes used instead of the traditional heavy timber roofs.*

Hippie centers like San Francisco's Haight-Ashbury district were besieged by tourists, hassled by the police, and torn up by drugs, violence, and disease. Many of the hippies of the day fled the cities and tried to take up life anew in the countryside.

At first these communes were little more than rural crash pads. They took put-on names like Drop City. There was rarely a stable population or any thought of the future. The Hog Farm was a traveling commune that moved from place to place in its psychedelically-painted buses. Mobility and formlessness were characteristic of these early communes. The communalists lived by working part-time, scrounging, getting welfare payments and food stamps, or on income provided by parents or a monied member of the group. But the desire to start something more permanent took hold as the movement began to spread across the country. City-bred kids started taking a serious interest in farming. People who had always lived in apartments started building cabins or other sorts of shelters in the country. Although the commune phenomenon remains primarily a youthful one, some older people, fleeing the pressures of urban or suburban living, have joined communes or started them.

In the past the poor had often joined communes to raise their standard of living, for in the nineteenth century successful communitarians generally lived better than they might otherwise have expected to. Today the situation is radically different. The modern commune movement is made up primarily of middle-class people. Those who move out of the mainstream and onto a commune have made a deliberate decision to lower their standard of living, often drastically. They have turned their backs on the material success that is so much a part of "the American Way of Life."

Although the reasons for an individual joining a commune are almost as varied as the number of individuals living on communes, most hold a few common ideals, goals, and dislikes. The one thing that all communitarians share is profound dissatisfaction with "the American Way of Life"—the idea of getting ahead, no matter what the cost, of making money, acquiring more objects and more status. Many of the older communalists have given up high-paying jobs and expensive homes to get out of what they call the rat race. Many of the younger ones have gone from college to commune, bypassing the rat race entirely, often to the horror of their parents.

A second common theme is the desire to "groove with nature." The commune movement and the ecology movement are closely connected. Most communes try to engage in organic gardening and preparing natural foods. There is great stress laid upon physical, as opposed to intellectual, labor. Some communalists also hope to achieve some sort of mystical rapport with nature.

Still another common desire of modern communalists is to find new and more satisfying forms of interpersonal relationships. They feel that the monogamous marriage and the small nuclear family are no longer viable institutions. They stress that in the past people lived in large family groups. Grandparents, uncles, aunts, and cousins, all depended upon one another and supported one another. Child raising was carried on by the entire extended family rather than by the parents alone. Today most people live in a family unit consisting of a mother, a father, and children, with only occasional visits from other relatives. This, say the communitarians, is not enough. In the commune they hope to reestablish the security of the extended family. Some even talk of developing a new sense of tribalism.

Many outsiders believe the commune is a hotbed of promiscuous sex and drug abuse. Although widespread, sex and drugs play lesser roles in modern communes than popularly supposed. Sexual relations in communes run the gamut. In some of the hip communes impersonal sexual promiscuity is the rule; other communities have experimented with forms of group marriage, while in others old-fashioned monogamy is practiced. Generally, free-love communes do not last very long. Often they are torn apart by the very feelings of jealousy and exclusivity that the communalists hoped to escape.

Celibacy is not popular with modern communalists as it was with those of the nineteenth century, but in some groups sexual relations are severely controlled. Among the thousand or so members of the Hare Krishna sect, all sexual relations, including kissing, are considered illicit unless performed between married couples once a month at the optimum time for procreation. Intercourse is attempted only after each partner performs several hours of repetitive chanting to cleanse the mind.

One of the attractions of the early hip communes was that they were places where one could use drugs without being bothered by the police. Today many communalists say that they were first "turned on" to the communal way of life after an experience with LSD or some other psychedelic drug. But most stable communes now tolerate only "soft" drugs, like marijuana, or ban drug use entirely. There are two primary reasons for this new prohibition. First, keeping a commune together is physically hard enough; it is impossible if everyone is sitting around getting stoned. Second, since outside authorities are generally hostile to communes, the quickest way to break them up is to arrest the members on drug charges. The use of drugs also runs counter to the desire for natural living that many communalists feel. Some people say that since they have joined a commune, they no longer need drugs.

The religious element of the current communal revival is substantial—just how substantial depends upon one's definition of religion. Few of today's communes are directly connected with any established church. Some, like the fundamentalist Children of God (to be discussed in more detail shortly), are Christian sectarians as were most nineteenth century communalists. There are also communes that practice Buddhism or some other recognizable Oriental religion. The majority of communes have no particular religious system, but explore a range of religious and mystical ideas from Christianity to astrology, from ESP to a sort of pantheistic nature worship. There is even a commune dedicated to witchcraft.

Most modern communitarians reject rationalism and traditional religious structures and, as in the past, tend to rely upon individual inspiration and illumination. Such beliefs should lead to equalitarian religious and organizational systems, but they don't. As has happened time and again, inspiration and illumination usually encourage the development of charismatic leaders who can gain total power over their followers.

Certainly the most infamous of these leaders is Charles Manson, whose "family" was convicted of the grisly murder

*Hare Krishna members with spiritual master A. C.
Bhaktivedanta Swami Prabhupada (RIGHT) at the group's
West Virginia Farm.*

of actress Sharon Tate and six other people in California. Although no other commune leader has displayed such murderous instincts, Manson is by no means the only leader thought to possess divine powers. Most of these "divine" leaders tend to be benign and peaceful, but a few are rather bizarre.

Perhaps the most controversial commune leader active today is Mel Lyman, a former rock musician, whose "fam-

*Mel Lyman, from an altered photograph emphasizing his claims of divinity.*

ily" occupies houses in Boston, New York, and San Francisco, and has recently purchased a farm in Kansas. The Lyman family is not large, but because it has attracted a few wealthy members, it is well financed. The control that Lyman exercises over his family members is legendary in hip circles.

Lyman claims that he is Christ returned. One issue of a Lyman publication called *Avatar* contained a picture of a grinning Lyman sitting lotus position and floating among the stars with a drink in one hand and a halo above his head. The caption read in part:

"Hi, gang, I'm back, just like the book says. By God here I am, in all my glory, I thought I'd never come. But I'm here now and getting ready to do the good work. Maybe some of ya think I ain't Him. You'll see. I ain't about to prove it for you, much too corny. I'm Him and there just ain't no question about it. . . . So while most of you turn your heads and continue sticking to your silly romantic beliefs I'll let the rest of you in on a little secret. I'm Christ, I swear to God in *person*, and I'm about to turn this foolish world upside down. . . ."

Lyman's Christ claim is obviously something of a put-on, but the line between put-on and belief can be a very indistinct one. Those who have investigated the Lyman family closely testify that he is indeed regarded as a messiah or a god by his followers.

Communal energies tend to be directed inward toward the community itself; therefore, most communitarians engage in little political action, though their personal views may be quite radical. Many communalists have fled from radical political activity to the relative peace of communal life. However, in the current revival there are a few political communes. Some of them were inspired by opposition to the war in Vietnam. These communitarians were convinced that group solidarity was necessary for a long struggle against the war or other political evils. A few of these resistance communes have grown out of traditional pacifist groups like the Quakers. Others have formed around a specific project like publishing a newspaper or operating a peace center.

A tiny percentage of communes are distinctly revolutionary. Of these communitarians the Weathermen (or Weatherpeople, as they were renamed) are the most violent. The Weathermen, who have taken credit for bombings and other terroristic activities, formed communes primarily for mutual protection. The group received a great deal of publicity in 1969 and 1970, particularly when several of their members were killed in an explosion while making bombs in a Greenwich Village townhouse. As revolutionaries, the Weathermen are naturally secretive, and it is impossible to know how large the group is today, or for that matter, if it still exists at all.

Rarer even than the political commune in the current revival is what might be called the scientific utopian commune, on the Owen or Fourier model. Modern communes are largely antiscientific and antirational, and thus they are hostile to elaborate plans. The only major exceptions are the communities based upon the theories of B. F. Skinner. In 1948 Skinner, a Harvard University psychologist, wrote an account of a fictional modern utopia called *Walden Two*. Skinner's theories are too complicated to be summarized briefly, but basic to his philosophy is the belief that human behavior can be externally conditioned, and that by proper conditioning people can be made better. Skinner's utopia, however, was not a grim place of rewards and punishments, for Skinner believed that punishment was largely ineffective in changing long-term human behavior. Rather than punishing incorrect behavior, he advocated "positive reinforcement," or rewarding correct behavior.

Skinner himself has never shown much interest in founding a community based on his principles, but his book had an impact on college campuses, and several communities based loosely on the *Walden Two* model were formed.

The oldest and most impressive of these is Twin Oaks, founded in the mid-1960s and located near Louisa, Virginia. Unlike most modern communes, Twin Oaks does not reject technology, though the members acknowledge that excessive technology can be destructive and dehumanizing. The community runs a hammock factory that makes a small profit.

The work at Twin Oaks is conducted on a labor credit system. The community decides what jobs are to be done, and the people sign up for the jobs they wish to do. Jobs that are disagreeable and that few people sign up for are awarded a larger number of labor credits, and each community member is required to work off his or her share of labor credits. The system is reminiscent of the nineteenth century phalanxes. A unique feature is that work can be done at any time of the day or night.

Theoretically, the community's children are to be raised by the entire community under the direction of a child raising manager, and the communitarians aim toward the goal of eliminating the biological family as a social unit. But so far childbearing within the community has been discouraged until Twin Oaks is established on a firmer basis.

The problem of sexual relations at Twin Oaks has not been solved. There are no fixed rules about who sleeps with whom, and observers report that the community "operates on a more or less monogamous couple pattern of sexual relationships. One member said that the main reason thus far that people left the community is that they were unable to establish satisfactory sexual relations."

Interpersonal difficulties are suppressed as much as possible, for the residents at Twin Oaks feel that gossiping and grumbling about others can be extremely destructive in a small community. Twin Oaks is also highly selective about who can join, and potential members can be blackballed, even after completing the three-month probationary period.

Yet for all its admirable organization and planning, Twin Oaks is tiny. It has barely over two dozen members. Nor is the community truly self-supporting. Some of the members work outside the community and contribute their wages to it. Without such outside income, Twin Oaks could not survive, and even with it, the community's financial position is always precarious.

As indicated by this brief summary, the modern commune movement is a complicated phenomenon. In the pages that follow, we are going to look at a pair of modern communes. They cannot be regarded as typical, average, or representative communes, for in such a large, varied, and fluid movement, nothing is really typical, average, or representative. Each has some characteristics in common with other communes, and many differences. But, by looking at these two examples in greater detail, we may be able to convey some of the feel of what the modern commune movement is all about and how it operates.

# 8 🌿 The Children of God

The communities of the Children of God are very modern and yet in two important ways very traditional. First, the COGs, as they are often called, are fundamentalist Christians who, like many of the nineteenth century communalists, trace their way of life back to the Age of the Apostles, as described in the Book of Acts. Second, the COGs are profoundly apocalyptic; they deeply and sincerely expect the world to come to an end within their own lifetime.

Currently, the Children of God claim some three thousand members. They have fifty or sixty communes, or colonies, as they prefer to call them, scattered throughout the United States, a dozen or so in Europe, and a handful in South and Central America. The number and location of the communities change almost daily. Many of the colonies are simply rented apartments where a team of six to ten members of the sect live. The largest colony, now defunct, was a Texas ranch that accommodated over three hundred people.

The Children of God grew out of the Jesus movement, an attempt to bring fundamentalist Christianity to young people, particularly young people who had in one way or another become alienated from traditional Christianity and straight society in general. The founder of the COGs is an enigmatic man named David Berg. Berg had been a small-time professional evangelist, as had his parents before him. In 1968 and 1969 Berg and his family began to collect a group of followers made up primarily of California hippie-types. They were the prototype of the "Jesus freaks."

For his followers Berg decreed "one hundred percent discipleship"—that is, they were to devote all of their time and all of their resources to the business of spreading the gospel. Such a demand makes a communitarian life almost a necessity. The COGs do not look upon themselves as part of any commune movement. To them, the communal life is secondary to the religious life, just as they believe it was for the Apostles.

For a while the group was centered on property owned by Fred Jordan, a popular Texas radio and television evangelist and one-time employer of David Berg. But in 1971 there was an unexplained break between Berg and Jordan, and the Children of God scattered from the Texas ranch and spread across the country.

At about the time of the break Berg dropped out of public view entirely. Most of the members of the Children of God have never seen him and know practically nothing about him. Berg is believed to be living in a village somewhere in England, but even his family denies that they know exactly where he is. Contradictory reasons have been given for his secretiveness. Berg has written that he has a serious heart condition and cannot tolerate the excitement that publicity would bring. Still, David Berg, calling himself Moses, effectively controls the Children of God from his hiding place. His letters, signed MO for Moses, carry absolute authority within the group, and his wife, sons, daughters, and some of their spouses are the primary spokesmen of the COGs. In private COG "elders" refer to the Bergs as "the Royal Family."

*The Children of God leader called Watchman plays for a meeting at the Ellenville, New York colony.*

Berg's doctrine of one hundred percent discipleship has proved highly controversial. The parents of many of his young converts claim that they have not been allowed to see or otherwise communicate with their children and that the sect teaches children to hate their parents. The COGs deny this, but they often quote Jesus' statement in the tenth chapter of Matthew:

"Think not that I am come to send peace on earth: I came not to send peace, but a sword. For I am come to set a man at variance against his father, and the daughter against her mother, and the daughter in law against her mother in law. And a man's foes shall be they of his own household."

Unhappy parents formed a national parents committee called Free Our Children from the Children of God, better known as FREECOG. The COGs themselves call the group KILLCOG. FREECOG has held national conferences in which the Children of God have been denounced as "a Satanic force." They have brought various legal actions against the group and have pressured some local authorities into moving against COG communities for health or other violations. COG has retaliated with a million dollar libel suit against FREECOG, and by encouraging the formation of a group of parents who like them. This organization is called Thankful Parents of the Children of God, or THANKCOG. COG has also given its members permission to have more contact with their parents, and has generally turned a friendlier face to the world. But the hostility between the COGs and many of their parents has not really diminished. COG colonies are regularly invaded by distraught or angry parents who accuse the group of having "kidnapped" and "brainwashed" their children. Parents have occasionally "kidnapped" their children back at gunpoint, had children committed to mental institutions, or jailed if they refused to leave the COGs willingly.

Another point of controversy surrounding the Children of God is the group's attitude toward America. Most fundamentalist groups are politically conservative, equating patriotism with Christianity. For this reason, conservatives are generally happy about the Jesus movement, because it seems to turn young people away from political and social action and toward "spiritual values." At first the COGs received support from conservative businessmen. But the COGs don't make conservatives comfortable anymore, for while they are religiously conservative in one sense, they are extremely radical in another. COG holds no political opinions as such, though the group's general outlook has been described as a mixture of Old Right and New Left. It is almost as though David Berg's conservative evangelistic philosophy has merged with the anarchistic and antiestablishment views of his young followers. COG holds that America is evil and will soon fall victim to civil strife, insurrection, and probably a Communist take-over. This will be God's judgement on the nation and part of the worldwide time of troubles that will precede the end of the world. Most of the members of COG are actively planning to follow their leader out of the country, for they expect persecution in America to rise sharply. Berg's writings on the subject exhibit a strong paranoid streak.

As communitarians, the COGs are as anticapitalist as they are anticommunist for religious reasons. In general, they reject and hate all of the conventions and values of straight society. They speak of themselves as radicals, and their rallying cry is "Revolution—for Jesus" with the word "Revolution" shouted most loudly. This makes them as alarming to the established churches as the early Shakers must have been.

Berg is also expecting all sorts of worldwide natural catastrophes before the end of the world. He left California in 1968 when he (and many others) believed that there was going to be a great earthquake in the state. When writing about this incident, Berg sounds a bit sorry that the earthquake never took place.

*The Labor Day 1972 open house at the Ellenville colony.*

All of these controversies seem very far away when one first visits a COG colony, as I did in the summer of 1972. This colony was located near the town of Ellenville in the Catskill Mountain region of New York. The property, which had once been a small resort, was leased to the COGs by a drug rehabilitation project that owned it. It consisted of a large main building, a motel unit, and several smaller buildings.

Berg has specifically warned his followers against buying property, lest they be tied down, so renting or borrowing is the rule. This colony housed between forty and sixty people and was one of the largest COG colonies at the time.

The Children of God had received a great deal of bad publicity at about the time I made my first visit. This particular colony was being heavily pressured to vacate by local authorities. I was a little uncertain of the reception I would get. Though I had arrived unannounced and unknown, the COGs couldn't have been friendlier or more helpful. I was allowed to go anywhere I pleased and to talk to anyone I wished, even new members. There were no restrictions on the kinds of questions I could ask, and no one got angry if some of the questions sounded suspicious or hostile. Though the answers were not always satisfactory, and were sometimes contradictory or evasive, at least there were answers, and the more one talked, the franker the answers became. Generally, no one talked to me alone; there were always at least two COGs in the room, and I was informed that this was a general rule. But even this practice was occasionally relaxed or forgotten.

One of the COGs that I met on my first visit said he was thirty-one years old. The majority were twenty or under, with a sprinkling of people in their late twenties. They adopted no distinctive style of dress. The men generally wore their hair long, and there was a fair percentage of beards and mustaches, but it was nothing one might not see on an average college campus, though the COGs seemed a bit neater. The women favored long bright-colored granny dresses and heavy oxford shoes. There were no mini-skirts or shorts. The most apparent difference between the COGs and any other group of young people was that the COGs always carried a Bible, sometimes on a strap slung across their shoulder like a purse.

The very informality of this community was strikingly different from the tightly structured communities of the nineteenth century. Everyone had plenty of time to sit around and chat—this indeed seemed to be their principal occupation. The love of work that had counted so heavily with the Shakers and other early communitarians was entirely absent among these modern commune members.

Everyone spoke of leading a life of sacrifice and discipline, but the COGs' schedule was not very rigorous. Members of the community rose at eight A.M., ate breakfast, and went to a Bible study class. The classes consisted mainly of reading selected portions of the Bible and interpreting them in light of the COG outlook on the world. Most of the newer members knew very little about the Bible, though they had all committed certain passages to memory, like the one quoted earlier from Matthew about families.

Around noon lunch was served in a common dining room. Meals were plain and leaned heavily toward cheap, filling foods like spaghetti, beans, and hot dogs, but no one looked undernourished.

After lunch there were two or three hours of chores—housecleaning, making necessary repairs, etc. Although the community was clean, it looked shabby; obviously no one made any more repairs than necessary. Work appeared to be assigned by the older members of the colony, with the harder jobs going to the new members.

When the chores were finished, the COGs drifted off to more meetings and classes. Visiting members or new members gave their "testimonies." On one of my visits I heard a member tell of his experiences during a trip through South America. Occasionally videotapes from some of the distant or foreign colonies were shown. (The COGs like electronic gadgets and cameras.) There was always a break to watch the six o'clock news on TV. The COGs almost seem to expect that some day the end of the world is going to be announced on the evening news. There was supper and then more meetings, some of which could go on until quite late. No rigid rules about bedtime were imposed in the community, as far as I could determine.

On weekends most of the members of the colony loaded into buses and headed for places where young people congregate. They often went to Greenwich Village in New York City or to rock concerts, state fairs, and the like. This they regarded as their main work, and it consisted primarily of singing and witnessing—that is, preaching and trying to make converts.

Expenses must have been fairly low considering the number of individuals who were being housed and fed, but still there was a need for some income, and no one in this community worked an outside job. How, I asked, did the community support itself? Finances turned out to be a touchy subject for the COGs. Often they replied with a shrug and said, "God provides." They also contended that much of their food comes from sympathetic businessmen who give them day-old bread and dented cans. Though they don't like to talk about it, it is clear that much of the money for the Children of God is provided, willingly or unwillingly, by the members and their parents. Members sign over to the group everything they own when they join; if this includes a car or a bank account, the sum can amount to several thousand dollars, even if the member had not been wealthy. "Most churches tithe their membership," one COG told me. "We don't bother with that; we take it all at once."

Parents often continue to send money to their sons and daughters who are members of COG. This too goes into the common pot. If parents do not send money, they can be subjected to fairly heavy pressure from their children or from other members of the sect to "contribute." The COGs have been accused of deliberately cultivating rich converts while ignoring their poorer brethren. Just who handles these contributions and what is done with the money is not clear.

Community members have to get special permission to

*A prayer meeting of the Children of God at their Ellenville colony.*

work at outside jobs, and such permission is given only when money is desperately needed. Unlike the Shakers, the COGs do not see work as a form of worship. To them the only meaningful form of work is God's work—that is, making converts. In his private communications Berg encourages his followers to get money where they can and when they can. To get contributions from conservative businessmen, the COGs play down their radical views and pose as ordinary Christian Bible students.

Another striking difference between this modern commune and those of the last century is the mobility of the membership. In the nineteenth century people with communitarian interests might try one group after another until they found a place that suited them and they settled down, or they abandoned the quest altogether. Among the COGs mobility is a deliberate policy. Again it was David Berg who set the tone: ". . . moving is one of our professions! We're Gospel Gypsies, having no certain resting place! This world is not our home. . . ."

Most of the COGs that I talked to had lived in a dozen or more of the sect's colonies within a single year. Most were anxiously looking forward to going to Europe or South America.

Upon joining the sect, members give up their names and take Biblical names like Jeremiah, Josiah, and the like. Often, they are reluctant to tell you the names they had before joining, but they are all anxious to give their "testimony" and tell you what sort of unhappy sinners they were before Jesus saved them, and they joined the COGs.

A small percentage of COGs at the Ellenville colony came from fundamentalist Christian backgrounds, and joined the group because they felt that the organized churches were not living up to the Bible. These are young people who had already accepted literal interpretation of the Bible as their only guide. The majority of COGs, however, had little or no

church background. They were dropouts from straight society. Many told of unhappy family lives and nightmarish
experiences with drugs. Neither the communal life nor the
wandering life was new to them. Most had lived on other
types of communes and had traveled ceaselessly. Few had
ever held regular jobs, and they were used to getting money
from their parents. The Children of God provides such individuals with a badly needed feeling of family and a purpose in life. The sect also helps them overcome any drug
problem they may have had. Even the COGs' worst enemies
admit that the group is drug free. For such members the
feeling of security, support, and community seemed far
more important than the Biblical interpretations offered by
the group. COG elders said proudly that until most of their
members had joined the sect, they had never known what
a family really was. Every COG that I talked to was absolutely convinced that he or she had made a lifetime commitment to the group.

The COGs win most of their converts out on the street,
though some people seek out the communes to join. Anyone
can become a member, and the trial period is only two
weeks. The new members, or babes, are given a rigorous in-
doctrination course in the Bible as interpreted by David
Berg. They are hardly ever left alone, read nothing but the
Bible, and often have posters containing select Biblical
phrases hung in their rooms. They are required to read and
reread the same Biblical passages until they have them
memorized. This has led to charges that the COGs somehow
hypnotize or brainwash their converts. Many of the babes,
however, never finish the two weeks, and the COGs suspect
that some come in just for the free meals. Even after the
two-week trial period the COGs acknowledge a dropout rate
of about twenty percent, and considering the number of ex-
COGs around, the dropout rate may be considerably higher.
Members who try to leave are subjected to heavy psycho-

logical pressure and are threatened with eternal damnation. But this is not unusual in Christian sects, or for that matter in conventional churches.

There are no officers elected or appointed in the Children of God. In fact, at first it is a little difficult to tell that the group has any leaders at all. The COGs tend to deny the principle of earthly leadership, saying rather that they rely upon the inspiration of God. But as in other groups that rely on divine inspiration, there are always those who are more inspired than others. In practice, authority runs from David Berg through his family to the older and more trusted members who are in every colony. The babes have no part in the decision-making, and are usually unaware that decisions are being made for them.

Sex is a subject the COGs do not like to discuss frankly. Men outnumbered women in the Ellenville community three or four to one. Except for Berg's own daughters, men hold all the power. The COGs have appropriate Biblical quotes to justify this situation. The COGs claim that they believe in monogamous marriage, but their opponents contend that this is not true and that various members are assigned different sexual partners. Some of David Berg's writings seem to indicate that COG sexual practices are less than traditional. As John Humphrey Noyes proved, the Bible can be used to justify all manner of sexual relations.

The COGs do not believe in birth control, and at the colony I visited eighty percent of the women were either pregnant or caring for infants. Older children were cared for by the women of the community in general, rather than by their own mothers exclusively. The children at the Ellenville commune were well treated and looked happy. In some cases the children were close to their biological parents; in other cases the parents did not appear to be in the community at all. Education had not yet become a problem because the sect had not been in existence long enough for any of the children born into it to be school-age, and few couples who already had children have joined. The presence of children, however, has increased the strains between many COG members and their own parents, who wish to rescue their grandchildren from the COGs.

The COGs also do not believe in having their children in hospitals, so almost all babies are born in the colony, with only other community members assisting. One of their newspapers carried a cartoon strip showing how to deliver a baby. They claim that in over ninety-five percent of the cases they had not been required to call for medical aid.

David Berg described the Children of God as people on the bottom, "a peculiar people, despised, rejected, and hated of all men!" That is perhaps too strong a description, but certainly the COGs are not popular today. At the Ellenville colony the group held an open house on Labor Day. Though the weather was perfect, there was plenty of free food and a free rock concert, and the group had received a lot of publicity to stimulate local curiosity, practically no one aside from members showed up. "It's typical," one of the leaders told me. "People criticize us, but they don't even come to see us. What do they think that we are going to do, drug their food? Hypnotize them? Who do they think we are, the Manson family?"

Still, the COGs enjoyed the afternoon. They sang and danced on the lawn and presented skits, just as they do on street corners. The few visitors were treated with elaborate politeness and were assured time and again that Jesus loved them. It was all very idyllic, very theatrical, and very unreal. The songs and skits carried a strong undercurrent of hatred for "the system." It is the same feeling that runs through David Berg's writing. There is much talk of love, but the driving emotion is hate. "We can say things in songs and skits that we wouldn't want to say flat out," a leader informed me.

A few days after their open house the COGs were gone. Their colony had been cited for building violations, and

*The COGs prepare to depart from their Ellenville colony.*

their lease was running out. Local officials had been contacted by a California state official who has been going around the country warning people about the dangers of the COGs. The sheriff had invaded the community looking for a runaway.

The COGs could easily have fought the eviction, and perhaps have won. Certainly they could have obtained a stay of eviction. But they chose not to fight. Rather, they packed up their belongings, loaded up their buses, and scattered to other colonies.

On their former residence they left two signs, one from the New Testament:

"If they receive you not, depart and say: Even the very dust of your city which cleaveth on us, we do wipe off against you. Verily I say unto you it shall be more tolerable for the land of Sodom and Gomorrah in the Day of Judgement than for that city. Inasmuch as Ye have done it unto one of the least of these, my brethren, Ye have done it unto me."

Another smaller sign hung nearby and summed up the COGs' apocalyptic philosophy:

"Warning: Turn your eyes toward Memphis [Egypt] for out of it shall come the Great Confusion. The author of confusion is even now marshalling his forces for this Great Confusion. He is gathering his forces from a great nation and eastern nations, friends that will join with him. So sudden will be the Great Confusion that it will cause a widening of the eyes of those who have not discerned the signs of the times.

"But be ye not deceived. Be prepared. And be not deceived by the Great Society, for it will come to travail and then bring forth the Great Confusion. Be prepared. Even now the signs are red-red with warning and black-black with clouds gathering for the Great Confusion which is almost upon you."

Upon departing, one of the COG leaders told me, "I predict a very cold winter for Ellenville." It was almost like a curse.

# 9 🌿 The Manor

"Moving to a commune didn't seem like a radical step in my life," Peter, the young communalist, told me. "Maybe it was, but it came about by a series of small natural steps. I come from a large, close family with a lot of insanity. That's pretty much what it's like here. When I went to college, I lived in the dorms with roommates. After I graduated, I lived in an apartment with roommates, and when I moved out here, it first seemed like just a different set of roommates. Not so different either, because a couple of my old college roommates are living out here, too."

"Here" was a commune that didn't really have a name. The communitarians were living on a lovely, but somewhat rundown colonial estate in a rural area in upstate New York. Most of the people called the place the Manor.

The commune didn't own the property. Some members paid rent to live there, while others lived rent free with the understanding that they would look after the property and repair some of the buildings that had fallen into ruin. The owner was a college professor teaching in the Midwest, and he rarely visited the place. In the two years since the commune began, the Manor had been converted from a barely habitable collection of buildings to a very comfortable and attractive place.

There is a core of about ten people who have been with this commune from the beginning. Generally, anywhere from fourteen to twenty people could be found living at the Manor at any one time. They were all in their early twenties. Some would go off for a week or a month and then return. There are no firm rules about joining the commune. People just come and stay if they like it.

The commune at the Manor has no particular leaders, no established way of sharing work or finances, no organized way of handling disputes, not even any long-term goals. Yet somehow the group stays together. The commune was over two years old when I visited it, and considering the life-span of the average modern commune, the Manor was practically middle-aged. It was a robust middle age, too, for there seemed no reason why this group should break up before their lease on the Manor property ran out in about three years.

Although, as I have said, there is really no such thing as a typical, average, or representative commune, the communalists at the Manor are very ordinary sorts of people.

Peter, like most of the others, had come from a comfortable middle-class background. He and some of his friends had founded the commune. After he married, his wife, Rita, also came to the Manor, and she in turn brought two of her friends from school. Practically everyone at the Manor had come directly or almost directly from college. None had lived the wandering hippie life that had been so common in the background of the COGs. Several of the commune members were still attending college at a nearby branch of the state university.

The stereotype of modern communalists as sick or rebellious kids cannot be applied to this group. They didn't seem to have any more than the usual number of personal

*The Manor, home for an informal group of young communalists.*

maladjustments. Most said they got on well with their parents, and in fact, parents were frequent visitors at the Manor. Joining a commune, to these young people, was a natural, indeed an almost inevitable, step in their lives.

Like almost every other modern commune, the Manor was not self-supporting. Some of the members worked at outside jobs, usually menial and low-paying ones. Those who were students continued to receive money from their parents. But the total cash intake at the Manor was not very great, and expenses had to be kept as low as possible.

Farming or, more properly, gardening was one of the methods of saving money. There were a couple of fairly well-tended organic gardens in back of the houses, but this attempt at agriculture wasn't nearly as extensive as it might have been. I suspect that the primary motive for the gardening was a romantic desire to get back to the land, rather than a practical need for food. A single cow provided the communalists with more milk than they needed, and they were experimenting with making cheese. A few chickens were around, though they were poor layers, so most eggs were store-bought. There were also a couple of goats and horses, because someone liked goats and horses. In addition, the Manor supported a large population of wandering dogs and cats.

The Manor communitarians were better mechanics and builders than they were farmers. One of the men could repair practically any type of car; another was a skilled carpenter. On one of my visits, three of the men were installing a complicated-looking plumbing system in a building that they had renovated.

The women made most of their own clothes, and some were expert dressmakers. Though men did help with the dishes and cleaning up, the work of the commune was still pretty clearly divided between "men's work" and "women's work." The Manor had not yet experienced the women's liberation revolt that had shaken many of the more radical communes in 1971 and 1972.

Vegetarianism was the general rule at the Manor. Some of the people didn't eat meat from the moral conviction that it was wrong to eat animal flesh; others, because they thought vegetarianism was healthier; but the majority didn't eat meat because meat was too expensive. To keep a vegetarian diet from becoming too bland and boring, as well as to save money, a great deal of time was spent preparing and cooking food. Commercial bread was rarely used, though people bought cakes and pies when they could afford them. Fruits and vegetables from the garden were canned for the winter. Many of the traditional kitchen practices of the nineteenth century were being rediscovered by these twentieth century city-bred young people.

All of this might give the impression that the Manor was the scene of bustling activity, worthy of the Shakers. But the visitor gets quite the opposite impression. The communalists spent a lot of time watching television, playing cards or other games, reading (generally, things like science fiction or comic books), or just plain sitting around not doing much of anything. The horror of idleness that tormented generations of hardworking Americans had disappeared completely among these late twentieth century descendants.

"Sometimes people think that commune life is just one long orgy of drugs and sex. They should come and spend a few days with us to find out how boring and conventional it is most of the time," Peter observed.

Drugs were rarely used at the Manor. I was told that marijuana was available if I really wanted any, but that no one smoked it regularly. There was no moral prohibition against pot; people just didn't bother with it. The worst addiction found at the Manor was to ordinary cigarettes. Several of the communalists were heavy smokers and were trying heroically to break the habit.

Casual sexual promiscuity, which outsiders so often associate with communal living, was not a part of life at the Manor either. "They all think we sleep in the same bed and take the same bath," one communalist told me, "but it just isn't so."

When I visited the Manor, men outnumbered women two to one. This ratio changes frequently, but there are usually more men than women. Peter and Rita were the only married couple in the group, but there were a couple of other fairly stable monogamous relationships. The communalists acknowledged, however, that the problem of sexual pairing did create occasional tensions within the group.

There were other sources of strain; worry over work or money and a whole variety of all-too-human irritations would put everybody on edge. "It's gotten really tense around here on very many occasions," said Rita, "but we just really all want to get along, and if you want to get along, no matter how tense it gets, you eventually remove whatever it is that is causing the tension, either by talking it out or just letting it fall away. Everybody wants to get along and stay together."

Anyone could drop in at the Manor and stay for a meal, a night, a week, or forever, if that's what he wanted to do. This sometimes put a strain on the food budget, and the communalists acknowledged that they did have a problem with freeloaders. But they insisted that anyone who refused to do his share of the work, or who for one reason or another didn't fit in, would not stay around for very long. No one had ever been physically expelled from the property. People just went away because they were made to feel very uncomfortable. Besides, the Manor wasn't easy to find in the first place. One needed a car and a good set of directions to get there. It was too far from towns or main roads for hitchhikers. If a person did get to the Manor, it was generally because someone who lived there had invited him.

The Manor was large enough for every individual or couple to have a separate room. There were no locks on the doors, and a good deal of casual dropping in without knocking went on. But anyone could get some privacy if he wished. This unusually favorable physical setup undoubtedly helped to keep interpersonal tensions and conflicts at a minimum. In most communes living conditions are considerably more cramped.

None of the Manor communalists that I talked to expressed any particular religious or spiritual motives for the style of life they had chosen. Some avowed a sort of vague faith in "a humanist kind of religion." They also expressed some of the currently fashionable interest in astrology, Oriental religions, mysticism, and more esoteric occult topics, but no one really knew too much about any of it, or for that matter, cared.

There was also a notable lack of enthusiasm about being part of a movement. These communalists knew very little about other communes, and though they expressed the belief that communal life was becoming more popular among the young today, they didn't regard themselves as pioneers of a new and better way of life. There wasn't a single book about communes in the large book collection, and no one subscribed to any of the publications about communes (though they did subscribe to *Playboy* and *The National Lampoon*). For the people of the Manor, the commune experience was almost entirely a personal one.

No one at the Manor felt the slightest need for elaborate justifications for the commune or fancy theories about how it should work. To them, it was a natural and good way to live. None of the communalists felt that communal living was going to sweep the country and completely transform America within a generation, but they did feel that it was becoming more and more acceptable. "At one time you had

OPPOSITE:
*Residents of the Manor as they appeared in a photograph on their 1972 Christmas card.*

to be pretty far out to join a commune," said Peter. "Most people dismissed the idea as absurd. Now people don't do that anymore. No one just dismisses the idea. You read in magazines how people have given up big executive positions to move out into the woods."

Peter said that a lot of people in their thirties had become very romantic about the communal idea. "Older people, in their forties and fifties, can't really consider changing. But people in their thirties, they figure that they are so close. If they could only shed the pattern of life that they aren't finding very satisfactory anyway, they might be able to make their way. Most of them can't change or won't, but a lot want to."

Money, although not worshipped at the Manor, was not scorned either. Peter figured that he and his wife would never need more than $10,000 or $15,000 a year, tops. I pointed out that such an income would place them well above the average American family. Peter countered by saying he had been used to a considerably higher income in his parents' home, and he could reasonably expect to have made a lot more if he had stayed inside the system, but he didn't think that getting a lot of money was worth the effort. "I don't want to be poor. But I don't need a whole lot of money to be happy either. I could probably make a lot if I went out into the business world, but I would be miserable. Who needs it?"

Perhaps the people at the Manor don't worry much about the future, or perhaps they just don't talk much about it. None of them seem to have any plans about what they are going to be doing in five or ten years. They talk vaguely of moving to some other commune, so that they can continue doing just about what they are doing now. There was only one child at the commune, and he had been born before his parents moved to the Manor. No one else seemed to be planning to have children. When asked why, Peter replied with a shrug that no one felt "ready" for children yet. When would they feel "ready"? What did "ready" mean? The answer was just a shrug this time.

Here, at the Manor, are college trained and often talented young people who spend much of their time doing menial tasks, and doing only enough of those to be able to lead a life of moderate comfort. Some might condemn these communalists for their almost total lack of traditional ambitions and goals. They might appear to be lazy and self-indulgent, a bunch of spoiled kids. But the Manor communalists simply don't have the work ethic of the Shakers and Rappites or the intellectual and social goals of the Brook Farmers and Perfectionists. Though they all hold vaguely liberal or even radical political views, they are not political activists, and care little for politics in general. They are not out to change the world; they simply want to be happy and to get along with one another. And at this, they do work terribly hard.

"Our parents and grandparents saw economic hard times," Peter explained. "They worked hard to better themselves economically. A lot of our generation has seen spiritual and emotional hard times. This is how we hope to better ourselves."

# 10 🌿 The Future

When you are living through a historical event, it is quite impossible to determine whether that event is one of history's turning points or just a minor footnote.

The modern commune movement has already been subjected to a staggering number of analyses. Whether the particular analyst thinks that the commune movement will endure or fade away has depended less on facts than on the analyst's own attitude toward communitarian living.

I long ago turned in my crystal ball for seeing the future, and can only offer some highly personal (and therefore biased) and rather contradictory comments on the future of the commune movement in America.

As a member of the over-thirty generation who often has trouble getting along with his own neighbors, it appears to me that long-term communitarian living is both undesirable and virtually impossible. The whole thrust of current life, particularly economic life, seems to be running against the success of small communal groups just as strongly as it has since the end of the nineteenth century. Certainly the fact that few, if any, of today's communes are self-supporting indicates that the economic problems of the commune are a long way from being solved.

Many young communitarians still depend heavily on parental support, but after a few years this source usually dries up. Government programs like food stamps and welfare have helped others, but a politician couldn't hope for an easier target than "getting the hippies off the welfare rolls," and these funds are already being restricted.

Most communes get along by maintaining an extremely low standard of living. This is bearable, and even romantic for a while. Surely no one in the world really needs wall-to-wall carpeting, two cars, and a swimming pool. But the desire for minimal comforts is likely to become almost overpowering. People live with extreme hardship only when they have no choice. The idea that a group can somehow or other "live off the land" is an impossible dream. One need only look at the plight of the small farmer in America to know just how dead that particular dream is.

The most successful American communes, the Shakers and the German societies, drew their strength from their religious convictions. The roots of these groups went back to the fervent religious beliefs of past centuries, and the communes failed when their religious ardor cooled. Despite much talk of religious revivals and spiritual reawakenings today, the latter half of the twentieth century is not an era in which religion plays a major part in most people's lives.

Much of the modern communitarian rationale is based upon the desire to find an alternate life-style, something to replace monogamy and the traditional family. Right now the traditional family is under attack from many quarters. The critics say that some of the original functions of families—economic security, education of children, mutual protection, and so forth—have been taken over by other institutions. The family, they contend, no longer has a place in the world, and that is why so many families are in deep trouble.

But as an alternative, the communal way obviously presents its own problems. The majority of communes don't last more than a few months, and disenchanted communitarians relate tales of jealousy, greed, and general human cussedness that make ordinary family life sound tranquil and satisfying by comparison. Even in stable communes the members have to spend an incredible amount of time and energy simply trying to get along with one another, and have precious little of either left to confront the many other difficulties of life.

When I totaled all of this up, I decided that the commune movement simply could not exist. And yet there it is, and it is growing.

As I talked to the members of the Children of God, I was struck by the thought that had I the opportunity to interview the followers of Jacob Hutter in the sixteenth century, I might have missed their resolve and seriousness of purpose too. The writings of COG founder David Berg often seemed little more than incoherent babblings to me. Yet that is exactly what many of Ann Lee's contemporaries thought of her ideas. Neither the Hutterites nor Ann Lee's Shakers changed the world, but they survived and provided an alternate life-style for thousands.

The greatest surprise I received was the way in which the communalists at the Manor, and other young people both on and off communes, accept the noncompetitive communal way of life as both a natural and desirable goal. Some students of human and animal behavior insist that competition is a basic biological drive. I certainly thought that it was when I was growing up. But the young communalists of today disagree, both in words and by the way that they live.

Although most modern communitarians are unclear as to what communal life should be, and are not particularly hopeful that the commune movement will survive the pressures from the outside world, they are remarkably unified on one thing—they reject the goals of success, be they material, social, or intellectual, which have driven their parents and grandparents. It is possible to put down this rejection as a case of youthful rebellion or the results of the generation gap, something that the communalists will grow out of. Perhaps that is so, but as yet there is no sign of a mass return to "the American Way of Life." Quite the reverse.

I recalled the statement made by an unnamed critic of the Shakers, who contended that Americans would never join communes because "We Americans are a go-ahead people, not to be confined anywhere or stopped by anything." The statement was made about a century ago, and it sounds hopelessly out of date now. Maybe America really has changed. Many of us have found that simply "going ahead" isn't very fulfilling anymore, and we have begun to turn inward and search for different and more satisfying ways to live.

# Suggestions for Further Reading

Those books marked with an asterisk (*) are specifically meant for younger readers.

Andrews, Edward Deming. *The Gift To Be Simple: Songs, Dances and Rituals of the American Shakers*. New York: Dover, 1962.
————. *The People Called Shakers*. New York: Dover, 1963.
Bach, Marcus. *Strange Sects and Curious Cults*. New York: Dodd, Mead, 1961.
Bestor, Arthur Eugene, Jr. *Backwoods Utopias: The Sectarian and Owenite Phases of Communitarian Societies in America 1663–1829*. Philadelphia: University of Pennsylvania Press, 1950.
Cohn, Norman. *The Pursuit of the Millennium*. Fairlawn, N.J.: Essential Books, 1959.
*Hedgepeth, William, and Stock, Dennis. *The Alternative: Communal Life in New America*. New York: Collier, 1970.
Hinds, William Alfred. *American Communities*. Chicago: Charles H. Kerr Co., 1908.
Holloway, Mark. *Heavens on Earth* (Revised Edition). New York: Dover, 1966.
*Horwitz, Elinor Lander. *Communes in America: The Place Just Right*. Philadelphia: Lippincott, 1972.
Melcher, M. F. *The Shaker Adventure*. Princeton: Princeton University Press, 1941.
Melville, Keith. *Communes in the Counter Culture*. New York: Morrow, 1972.
*Morse, Flo. *Yankee Communes: Another American Way*. New York: Harcourt Brace, 1971.

Nordhoff, Charles. *The Communistic Societies of the United States.* New York: Dover, 1966.

Noyes, John Humphrey. *Strange Cults and Utopias of 19th Century America.* New York: Dover, 1966.

Roberts, Ron E. *The New Communes: Coming Together in America.* Englewood Cliffs, N.J.: Prentice-Hall, 1971.

 Index

## G

## H

# M